THE BRITANNICA GUIDE TO ISLAM

THE ISLAMIC WORLD TO 1041

EDITED BY ARIANA WOLFF

Britannica Educational Publishing
IN ASSOCIATION WITH
ROSEN EDUCATIONAL SERVICES

Published in 2018 by Britannica Educational Publishing (a trademark of Encyclopædia Britannica, Inc.) in association with The Rosen Publishing Group, Inc.
29 East 21st Street, New York, NY 10010

Distributed exclusively by Rosen Publishing.
To see additional Britannica Educational Publishing titles, go to rosenpublishing.com.

First Edition

Britannica Educational Publishing
J.E. Luebering: Director, Core Reference Group
Andrea R. Field: Managing Editor, Compton's by Britannica

Rosen Publishing
Ariana Wolff: Editor
Nelson Sá: Art Director
Brian Garvey: Series Designer
Tahara Anderson: Book Layout
Cindy Reiman: Photography Manager
Nicole diMella: Photo Researcher
Introduction and conclusion by Linda Baker.

Cataloging-in-Publication Data

Names: Wolff, Ariana, editor.
Title: The Islamic world to 1041 / edited by Ariana Wolff.
Description: New York : Britannica Educational Publishing in association with Rosen Educational Services, 2018. | Series: The Britannica guide to Islam | Includes bibliographic references and index.
Identifiers: ISBN 9781680486193 (library bound)
Subjects: LCSH: Islamic civilization. | Islam--History. | Islamic countries--History.
Classification: LCC DS35.63 I845 2018 | DDC 909'.09767--dc23

Manufactured in China

Photo credits: Cover NataliaMilko/Shutterstock.com; pp. 7, 25, 58, 61, 110 Pictures from History/Bridgeman Images; pp. 10, 48 Encyclopædia Britannica, Inc.; p. 12 Bavaria-Verlag; p. 14 DEA/G. Dagli Orti/DeAgostini/Getty Images; p. 19 frees/Shutterstock.com; p. 22 Issam Madkouk/arabianEye/Getty Images; p. 27 Blaine Harrington III/Corbis Documentary/Getty Images; pp. 29, 32 DeAgostini Picture Library/Getty Images; p. 36 Samet Guler/Shutterstock.com; p. 38 Photos.com/Thinkstock; p. 42 Ahmad Faizal Yahya/Shutterstock.com; p. 50 DEA/S. Vannini/DeAgostini/Getty Images; p. 53 Alexander Mazurkevich/Shutterstock.com; p. 63 Michael Freeman/Digital Vision/Getty Images; p. 68 New York Public Library/Science Source/Getty Images; pp. 73, 91 Album/Prisma/SuperStock; p. 77 Jean Soutif/Science Source; p. 81 epa european pressphoto agency b.v./Alamy Stock Photo; p. 83 San Diego Museum of Art, USA/Edwin Binney 3rd Collection/Bridgeman Images; p. 89 muratcankaragoz/Shutterstock.com; p. 97 Fuse/Thinkstock; p. 101 The Walters Art Museum/W.650.22B/CC0; p. 103 Edinburgh University Library, Scotland/With kind permission of the University of Edinburgh/Bridgeman Images; p. 108 Andia/Universal Images Group/Getty Images; back cover, pp. 3-5 background design javarman/Shutterstock.com; interior pages border design Azat1976/Shutterstock.com

CONTENTS

INTRODUCTION

In recent years Islam has been the focus of growing attention in the Western world. The religion is often misunderstood, all too often associated with terrorism and extremist beliefs. Unfortunately, such a skewed misunderstanding of Islam often leads to discrimination and violence against practitioners of the Islamic faith. However, Islam has a rich history, and it indeed shares much in common with the other major religions of the world—particularly with the other two Abrahamic religions, Judaism and Christianity. By examining Islam and its historical development, greater understanding of the modern religion can be achieved.

Islam traces its origins to the Nile-to-Oxus region, spanning the area between the Nile and the Amu Darya (formerly Oxus) rivers. The fertility of this area enabled some nomadic tribes to settle in one place to farm, raise livestock, and form communities. This first led to trading between communities and then later gave rise to major city-states along regular trade routes. It is in this context that we find the emergence of Islam's two Abrahamic predecessors: first Judaism and later Christianity.

In 570 CE, the Prophet Muhammad was born in Mecca, a major city-state on the Arabian Peninsula located at the intersection of two main trade routes. His father died before he was born, and his mother died when he was just six years old. Both parents had belonged to the Hāshim clan, a branch of the powerful Quraysh, the ruling tribe of Mecca, that also guarded its most sacred shrine, the Kaʿbah. After being raised by his grandfather, Muhammad married an older, wealthy Meccan woman, Khadījah bint Khuwaylid, when he was twenty-five years old. By the time he was thirty-five, he was a respected figure in Mecca.

Around this time, Muhammad began to make solitary spiritual journeys into the rough desert outside Mecca. He would pray, meditate, and receive mystical visions. It was during one of these sojourns into

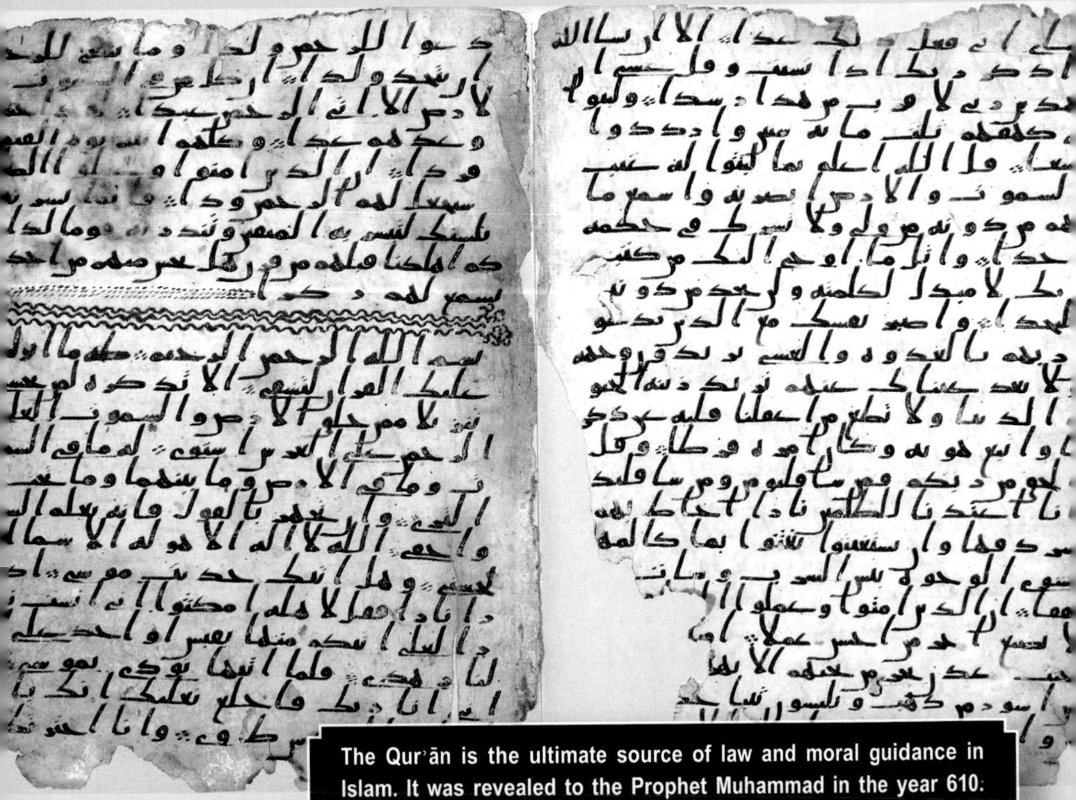

The Qur'ān is the ultimate source of law and moral guidance in Islam. It was revealed to the Prophet Muhammad in the year 610. Shown is the oldest surviving Qur'ānic manuscript, dated to before 645 CE.

the wilderness that Muhammad encountered the archangel Gabriel, who revealed to him the teachings that later came to make up the Qur'ān—Islam's holiest text.

As Muhammad gained followers, he also met with a great deal of opposition. Life for Muhammad and the early Muslims was difficult and dangerous as the result of extreme pressure exerted upon them by the Quraysh rulers of the city. In 622, Muhammad relocated to Yathrib, which became known as Madīnat al-Nabī ("City of the Prophet"), or Medina. The opposition that Muhammad and his followers faced only served to bring them closer together. In Medina, Muhammad focused on building the ideal society and building his community. Successful battles fought against the Quraysh only served to solidify early Islamic society.

Mohammad died in 632 without a successor. As with any new religion, controversies arose over leadership, belief, and behavior. By end of the millennium, Islam had spread extensively but was by no means cohesive. Differing local needs and approaches gave way to diversity in theology and practice. Despite such differences, the Qurʾān and records of the traditions or sayings of the Prophet Muhammad, known as Hadith, served as the major sources of law and moral guidance shared by all Islamic communities. In the 10th and 11th centuries Islam continued to grow and suffer controversy.

Chapter 1

Prehistory (c. 3000 BCE–500 CE)

The prehistory of Islamdom is the history of central Afro-Eurasia from Hammurabi of Babylon to the Achaemenid Cyrus II in Persia to Alexander the Great to the Sāsānian emperor Nūshīrvān to Muhammad in Arabia; or, in a Muslim view, from Adam to Noah to Abraham to Moses to Jesus to Muhammad. The potential for Muslim empire building was established with the rise of the earliest civilizations in western Asia. It was refined with the emergence and spread of what have been called the region's Axial Age religions—Abrahamic, centred on the Hebrew patriarch Abraham, and Mazdean (or Zoroastrian), focused on the Iranian deity Ahura Mazdā—and their later relative, Christianity. It was facilitated by the expansion of trade from eastern Asia to the Mediterranean and by the political changes thus effected. The Muslims were heirs to the ancient Egyptians, Babylonians, Persians, Hebrews, and even the Greeks and Indians; the societies they created bridged time and space, from ancient to modern and from east to west.

The Rise of Agrarian-Based Citied Societies

In the 7th century CE a coalition of Arab groups, some sedentary and some migratory, inside and outside the Arabian Peninsula,

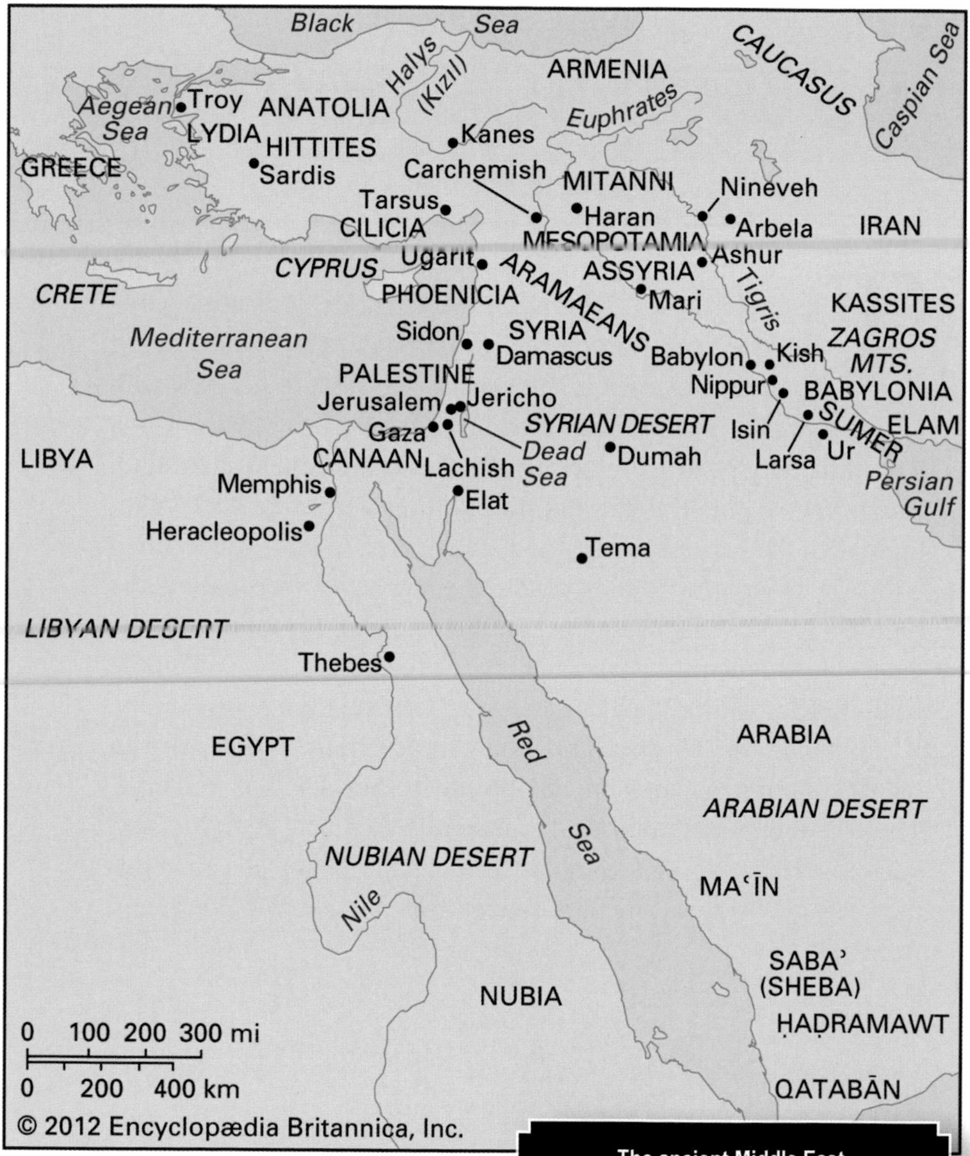

The ancient Middle East.

seized political and fiscal control in western Asia, specifically of the lands between the Nile and Oxus (Amu Darya) rivers—territory formerly controlled by the Byzantines in the west and the Sāsānians in the east. The factors that surrounded and directed their accomplishment had begun to coalesce long before, with the emergence of agrarian-based citied societies in western Asia in the 4th millennium BCE. The rise of complex agrarian-based societies, such as Sumer, out of a subsistence agricultural and pastoralist environment, involved the founding of cities, the extension of citied power over surrounding villages, and the interaction of both with pastoralists.

This type of social organization offered new possibilities. Agricultural production and intercity trading, particularly in luxury goods, increased. Some individuals were able to take advantage of the manual labour of others to amass enough wealth to patronize a wide range of arts and crafts; of these, a few were able to establish territorial monarchies and foster religious institutions with wider appeal. Gradually the familiar troika of court, temple, and market emerged. The new ruling groups cultivated skills for administering and integrating non-kin-related groups. They benefited from the increased use of writing and, in many cases, from the adoption of a single writing system, such as the cuneiform, for administrative use. New institutions, such as coinage, territorial deities, royal priesthoods, and standing armies, further enhanced their power.

In such town-and-country complexes the pace of change quickened enough so that a well-placed individual might see the effects of his actions in his own lifetime and be stimulated to self-criticism and moral reflection of an unprecedented sort. The religion of these new social entities reflected and supported the new social environments. Unlike the religions of small groups, the religions of complex societies focused on deities, such as Marduk, Isis, or Mithra, whose appeal was not limited to one small area or group and whose powers were much less fragmented. The relationship of earthly existence to the afterlife became more problematic, as evidenced by the elaborate death rites of pharaonic Egypt. Individual religious action began to compete with communal worship and ritual; sometimes it promised spiritual transformation and transcendence of a new sort, as illustrated in the pan-Mediterranean mystery religions. Yet large-scale organization had introduced social and economic injustices that rulers and religions could address but not resolve. To many, an absolute ruler uniting a plurality of ethnic, religious, and interest groups offered the best hope of justice.

Mithra slaying the bull, bas-relief, 2nd century CE; in the Städtisches Museum, Wiesbaden, Germany.

CULTURAL CORE AREAS OF THE SETTLED WORLD

By the middle of the 1st millennium BCE the settled world had crystallized into four cultural core areas: Mediterranean, Nile-to-Oxus, Indic, and East Asian. The Nile-to-Oxus, the future core of Islamdom, was the least cohesive and the most complicated. Whereas each of the other regions developed a single language of high culture—Greek, Sanskrit, and Chinese, respectively—the Nile-to-Oxus region was a linguistic palimpsest of Irano-Semitic languages of several sorts: Aramaic, Syriac (eastern or Iranian Aramaic), and Middle Persian (the language of eastern Iran).

THE NILE-TO-OXUS REGION

In addition to its various linguistic groups, the Nile-to-Oxus region also differed in climate and ecology. It lay at the centre of a vast arid zone stretching across Afro-Eurasia from the Sahara to the Gobi; it favoured those who could deal with aridity not only states that could control flooding (as in Egypt) or maintain irrigation (as in Mesopotamia) but also pastoralists and oasis dwellers. Although its agricultural potential was severely limited, its commercial possibilities were virtually unlimited. Located at the crossroads of the trans-Asian trade and blessed with numerous natural transit points, the region offered special social and economic prominence to its merchants.

The period from 800 to 200 BCE has been called the Axial Age because of its pivotal importance for the history of religion and culture. The world's first religions of salvation developed in the four core areas. From these traditions—for example, Judaism, Zoroastrianism, Buddhism, and Confucianism—derived all later forms of high religion, including Christianity and Islam. Unlike the religions that surrounded their formation, the Axial Age religions concentrated transcendent power into one locus, be it symbolized theistically or nontheistically. Their radically dualistic cosmology posited another realm, totally unlike the earthly realm and capable of challenging and replacing ordinary earthly values. The individual was challenged to adopt the right relationship with that "other" realm, so as to transcend mortality by earning a final resting place, or to escape the immortality guaranteed by rebirth by achieving annihilation of earthly attachment.

In the Nile-to-Oxus region two major traditions arose during the Axial Age: the Abrahamic in the west and the Zoroastrian in the east. Because they required exclusive allegiance through an individual confession of faith in a just and judging deity, they are called

The March of Abraham, painting by József Molnár, 19th century; in the Hungarian National Gallery, Budapest.

confessional religions. This deity was a unique all-powerful creator who remained active in history, and each event in the life of every individual was meaningful in terms of the judgment of God at the end of time. The universally applicable truth of these new religions was expressed in sacred writings. The traditions reflected the mercantile environment in which they were formed in their special concern for fairness, honesty, covenant keeping, moderation, law and order, accountability, and the rights of ordinary human beings. These values were always potentially incompatible with the elitism and absolutism of courtly circles. Most often, as for example in the case of the Achaemenian Empire, the conflict was expressed in rebellion against the crown or was adjudicated by viewing kingship as the guarantor of divine justice.

ZOROASTRIANISM

Zoroastrianism is an ancient Persian religion that was reformed during the 7th and 6th centuries BCE by a legendary figure named Zoroaster, or Zarathustra. Despite the rise and spread of Islam in Iran, beginning in the 7th century CE, Zoroastrianism has survived into the 21st century. The majority of its adherents live in India and are known as Parsis, which means "Persians." A lesser number still live in Iran, where they were until recently referred to as Gabars. The term gabar is derived from an Arabic word meaning "infidel." In the early 20th century, when wider religious tolerance was granted in Iran, the term ceased to be used.

Little is known of Zoroaster himself. He is said to have lived for 77 years during the 7th–6th centuries BCE. The prevailing religion of his time was a cult of many gods. He rejected all but one of them—Ahura Mazdā. The principle of evil was named Ahriman.

continued on the next page

continued from the previous page

A struggle between the two resulted in the creation of the world. Since its creation the whole world has been embroiled in the battle between good and evil, light and darkness.

Humanity, according to Zoroaster, is mortal and corrupted by Ahriman. Life, therefore, becomes a struggle by humans to embrace the light and avoid the darkness of evil. After death the soul crosses a bridge and passes either into heaven or hell. In later Zoroastrianism the end of the world was thought of as in the distant future. It was also believed that the souls of the damned would be purged so that they could share in the final renovation of the world.

Although modern Western historiography has projected an East-West dichotomy onto ancient times, Afro-Eurasian continuities and interactions were well established by the Axial Age and persisted throughout premodern times. The history of Islamdom cannot be understood without reference to them. Through Alexander's conquests in the 4th century BCE in three of the four core areas, the Irano-Semitic cultures of the Nile-to-Oxus region were permanently overlaid with Hellenistic elements, and a link was forged between the Indian subcontinent and Iran. By the 3rd century CE, crosscutting movements like Gnosticism and Manichaeism integrated individuals from disparate cultures. Similarly organized large, land-based empires with official religions existed in all parts of the settled world. The Christian Roman Empire was locked in conflict with its counterpart to the east, the Zoroastrian Sāsānian empire. Another Christian empire in East Africa, the Abyssinian, was involved alternately with each of the others. In the context of these regional interrelationships, inhabitants of Arabia made their fateful entrance into international political, religious, and economic life.

THE ARABIAN PENINSULA

The Arabian Peninsula consists of a large central arid zone punctuated by oases, wells, and small seasonal streams and bounded in the south by well-watered lands that are generally thin, sometimes mountainous coastal strips. To the north of the peninsula are the irrigated agricultural areas of Syria and Iraq, the site of large-scale states from the 4th millennium BCE. As early as the beginning of the 1st millennium BCE the southwest corner of Arabia, the Yemen, also was divided into settled kingdoms. Their language was a South Arabian Semitic dialect, and their culture bore some affinity to Semitic societies in the Fertile Crescent. By the beginning of the Common Era (the 1st century AD in the Christian calendar), the major occupants of the habitable parts of the arid centre were known as Arabs. They were Semitic-speaking tribes of settled, semi-settled, and fully migratory peoples who drew their name and apparently their identity from what the camel-herding Bedouin pastoralists among them called themselves: *ʿarab*.

Until the beginning of the 3rd century CE the greatest economic and political power in the peninsula rested in the relatively independent kingdoms of the Yemen. The Yemenis, with a knowledge of the monsoon winds, had evolved an exceptionally long and profitable trade route from East Africa across the Red Sea and from India across the Indian Ocean up through the peninsula into Iraq and Syria, where it joined older Phoenician routes across the Mediterranean and into the Iberian Peninsula. Their power depended on their ability to protect islands discovered in the Indian Ocean and to control the straits of Hormuz and Aden as well as the Bedouin caravanners who guided and protected the caravans that carried the trade northward to Arab entrepôts like Petra and Palmyra. Participation in this trade was in turn an important source of power for tribal Arabs, whose livelihood otherwise depended on a combination of intergroup raiding, agriculture, and animal husbandry.

By the 3rd century, however, external developments began to impinge. In the early 3rd century, Ardashīr I founded the Sāsānian empire in Fars; within 70 years the Sāsānian state was at war with Rome, a conflict that was to last up to Islamic times. The reorganization of the Roman Empire under Constantine the Great, with the adoption of a new faith, Christianity, and a new capital, Constantinople, exacerbated the competition with the Sāsānian empire and resulted in the spreading of Christianity into Egypt and Abyssinia and the encouraging of missionizing in Arabia itself. There Christians encountered Jews who had been settling since the 1st century, as well as Arabs who had converted to Judaism. By the beginning of the 4th century the rulers of Abyssinia and Ptolemaic Egypt were interfering in the Red Sea area and carrying their aggression into the Yemen proper. In the first quarter of the 6th century the proselytizing efforts of a Jewish Yemeni ruler resulted in a massacre of Christians in the major Christian centre of Najrān. This event invited Abyssinian Christian reprisal and occupation, which put a virtual end to indigenous control of the Yemen. In conflict with the Byzantines, the Zoroastrian Sāsānians invaded Yemen toward the end of the 6th century, further expanding the religious and cultural horizons of Arabia, where membership in a religious community could not be apolitical and could even have international ramifications. The connection between communal affiliation and political orientations would be expressed in the early Muslim community and in fact has continued to function to the present day.

The long-term result of Arabia's entry into international politics was paradoxical: it enhanced the power of the tribal Arabs at the expense of the "superpowers." Living in an ecological environment that favoured tribal independence and small-group loyalties, the Arabs had never established lasting large-scale states, only transient

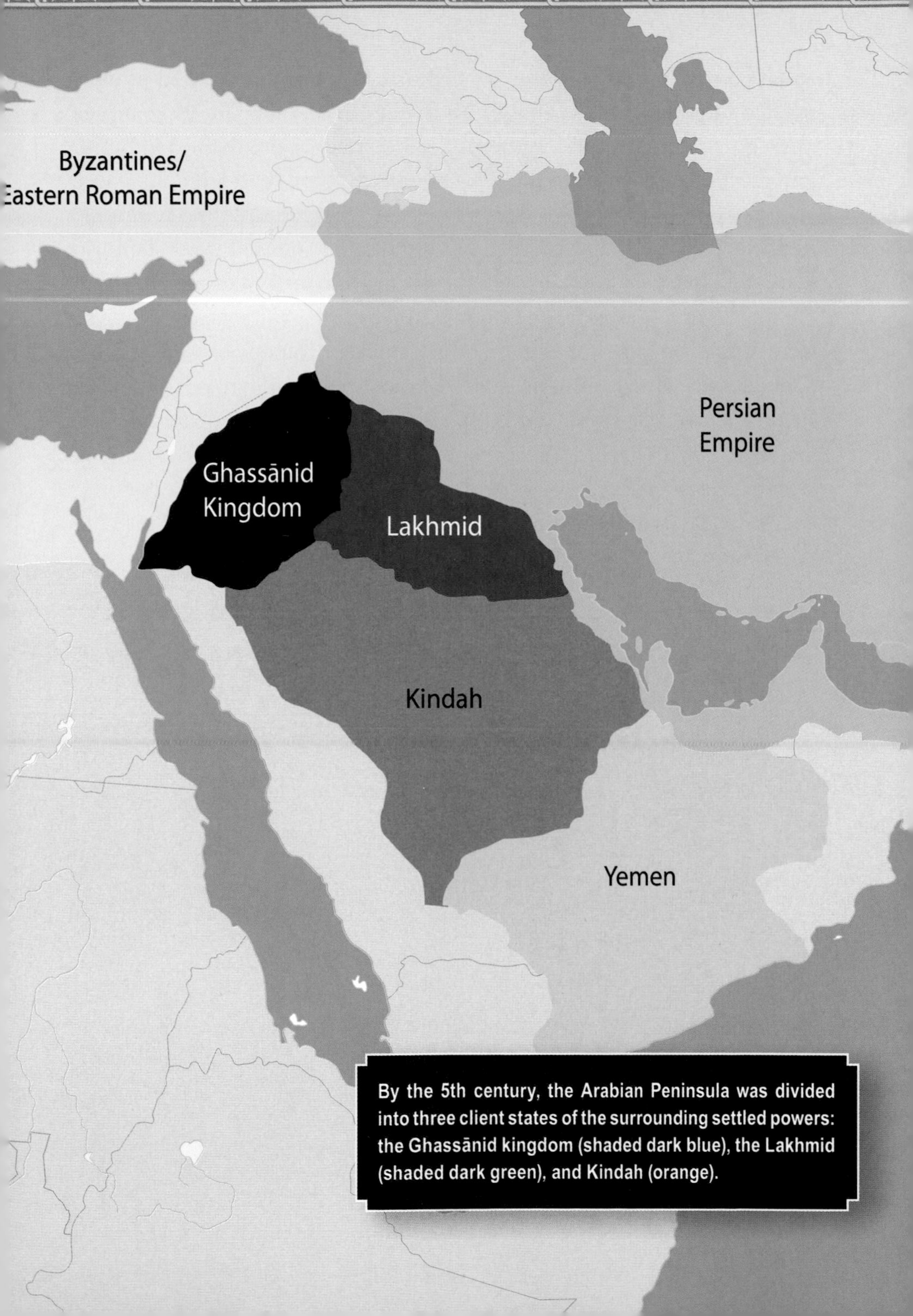

By the 5th century, the Arabian Peninsula was divided into three client states of the surrounding settled powers: the Ghassānid kingdom (shaded dark blue), the Lakhmid (shaded dark green), and Kindah (orange).

tribal confederations. By the 5th century, however, the settled powers needed their hinterlands enough to foster client states: the Byzantines oversaw the Ghassānid kingdom; the Persians oversaw the Lakhmid; and the Yemenis (prior to the Abyssinian invasion) had Kindah. These relationships increased Arab awareness of other cultures and religions, and the awareness seems to have stimulated internal Arab cultural activity, especially the classical Arabic, or *muḍarī*, poetry, for which the pre-Islamic Arabs are so famous. In the north, Arabic speakers were drawn into the imperial administrations of the Romans and Sāsānians; soon certain settled and semi-settled Arabs spoke and wrote Aramaic or Persian as well as Arabic, and some Persian or Aramaic speakers could speak and write Arabic. The prosperity of the 5th and 6th centuries, as well as the intensification of imperial rivalries in the late 6th century, seems to have brought the Arabs of the interior permanently into the wider network of communication that fostered the rise of the Muslim community at Mecca and Medina.

Chapter 2

Formation and Orientation (c. 500–634)

Although the 6th-century client states were the largest Arab polities of their day, it was not from them that a permanently significant Arab state arose. Rather, it emerged among independent Arabs living in Mecca (Makkah) at the junction of major north–south and west–east routes, in one of the less naturally favoured Arab settlements of the Hejaz (al-Ḥijāz). The development of a trading town into a city-state was not unusual, but, unlike many other western Arabian settlements, Mecca was not centred on an oasis or located in the hinterland of any non-Arab power. Although it had enough well water and springwater to provide for large numbers of camels, it did not have enough for agriculture; its economy depended on long-distance as well as short-distance trade.

Mecca under the Quraysh Clans

Sometime after the year 400 CE Mecca had come under the control of a group of Arabs who were in the process of becoming sedentary; they were known as Quraysh and were led by a man remembered as Quṣayy ibn Kilāb (called al-Mujammiʿ, "the Unifier"). During the generations before Muhammad's birth in about 570, the several clans of the Quraysh fostered a development in Mecca that seems to have been occurring in a few other Arab towns as well.

Despite its unusual location far from oases, Mecca developed into a major city-state. To this day, it remains the holiest of Muslim cities.

They used their trading connections and their relationships with their Bedouin cousins to make their town a regional centre whose influence radiated in many directions. They designated Mecca as a quarterly *ḥaram*, a safe haven from the intertribal warfare and raiding that was endemic among the Bedouin. Thus, Mecca became an attractive site for large trade fairs that coincided with pilgrimage (Arabic: *ḥajj*) to a local shrine, the Kaʿbah. The Kaʿbah housed the deities of visitors as well as the Meccans' supra-tribal creator and covenant-guaranteeing deity, called Allāh. Most Arabs probably viewed this deity as one among many, possessing powers not specific to a particular tribe; others may have identified this figure with the God of the Jews and Christians.

The building activities of the Quraysh threatened one non-Arab power enough to invite direct interference: the Abyssinians are said to have invaded Mecca in the year of Muhammad's birth. But the

THE KAʿBAH BEFORE ISLAM

The Kaʿbah is a small shrine located near the centre of the Great Mosque in Mecca. It is considered by Muslims everywhere to be the most sacred spot on Earth, however the structure predates Islam.

The early history of the Kaʿbah is not well known, but it is certain that in the period before the rise of Islam it was a polytheist sanctuary and was a site of pilgrimage for people throughout the Arabian Peninsula. The Qurʾān says of Abraham and Ishmael that they "raised the foundations" of the Kaʿbah. The exact sense is ambiguous, but many Muslims have interpreted the phrase to mean that they rebuilt a shrine first erected by Adam of which only the foundations still existed. The Kaʿbah has been destroyed, damaged, and subsequently rebuilt several times since.

The cube-shaped structure is roughly 50 feet (15 metres) high, and it is about 35 by 40 feet (10 by 14 metres) at its base. Constructed of gray stone and marble, it is oriented so that its corners roughly correspond to the points of the compass. The interior contains nothing but the three pillars supporting the roof and a number of suspended silver and gold lamps. During most of the year the Kaʿbah is covered with an enormous cloth of black brocade, the *kiswah*.

Located in the eastern corner of the Kaʿbah is the Black Stone of Mecca, whose now-broken pieces are surrounded by a ring of stone and held together by a heavy silver band. According to tradition, this stone was given to Adam on his expulsion from paradise in order to obtain forgiveness of his sins.

Byzantines and Sāsānians were distracted by internal reorganization and renewed conflict; simultaneously the Yemeni kingdoms were declining. Furthermore, these shifts in the international balance of power may have dislocated existing tribal connections enough to make Mecca an attractive new focus for supra-tribal organization, just as Mecca's equidistance from the major powers protected its independence and neutrality.

The Meccan link between shrine and market has a broader significance in the history of religion. It is reminiscent of changes that had taken place with the emergence of complex societies across the settled world several millennia earlier. Much of the religious life of the tribal Arabs had the characteristics of small-group, or "primitive," religion, including the sacralization of group-specific natural objects and phenomena and the multifarious presence of spirit beings, known among the Arabs as jinn. Where more-complex settlement patterns had developed, however, widely shared deities had already emerged, such as the "trinity" of Allāh's "daughters" known as al-Lāt, Manāt, and al-ʿUzzā. Such qualified simplification and inclusivity, wherever they have occurred in human history, seem to have been associated with other fundamental changes—increased settlement, extension and intensification of trade, and the emergence of lingua francas and other cultural commonalties, all of which had been occurring in central Arabia for several centuries.

New Social Patterns among the Meccans and Their Neighbors

The sedentarization of the Quraysh and their efforts to create an expanding network of cooperative Arabs generated social stresses that demanded new patterns of behaviour. The ability of the Quraysh to solve their problems was affected by an ambiguous relationship between sedentary and migratory Arabs. Tribal Arabs could go in and out of sedentarization easily, and kinship ties often transcended lifestyles.

Stone relief from Hatra depicting al-Lāt (*center*) flanked by two other figures, likely Manāt and al-ʿUzzā, 1st century CE.

The sedentarization of the Quraysh did not involve the destruction of their ties with the Bedouin or their idealization of Bedouin life.

Thus, for example, did wealthy Meccans, thinking Mecca unhealthy, often send their infants to Bedouin foster mothers. Yet the settling of the Quraysh at Mecca was no ordinary instance of sedentarization. Their commercial success produced a society unlike that of the Bedouin and unlike that of many other sedentary Arabs. Whereas stratification was minimal among the Bedouin, a hierarchy based on wealth appeared among the Quraysh. Although a Bedouin group might include a small number of outsiders, such as prisoners of war, Meccan society was markedly diverse, including non-Arabs as well as Arabs, slave as well as free. Among the Bedouin, lines of protection for in-group members were clearly drawn; in Mecca, sedentarization and socioeconomic stratification had begun to blur family responsibilities and foster the growth of an oligarchy whose economic objectives could easily supersede other motivations and values. Whereas the Bedouin acted in and through groups and even regularized intergroup raiding and warfare as a way of life, Meccans needed to act in their own interest and to minimize conflict by institutionalizing new, broader social alliances and interrelationships. The market-shrine complex encouraged surrounding tribes to put aside their conflicts periodically and to visit and worship the deities of the Kaʿbah; but such worship, as in most complex societies, could not replace either the particularistic worship of small groups or the competing religious practices of other regional centres, such as al-Ṭāʾif.

Very little in the Arabian environment favoured the formation of stable large-scale states. Therefore, Meccan efforts at centralization and unification might well have been transient, especially because they were not reinforced by any stronger power and because they depended almost entirely on the prosperity of a trade route that had been formerly controlled at its southern terminus and could be controlled elsewhere in the future, or exclude Mecca entirely. The rise of the Meccan system

As the Quraysh became sedentary in Mecca, they maintained ties to the migratory Bedouin and idealized their lifestyle. Shown are a Bedouin father and son crossing the Arabian Desert in Wadi Rum, Jordan.

also coincided with the spread of the confessional religions, through immigration, missionization, conversion, and foreign interference. Alongside members of the confessional religions were unaffiliated monotheists, known as *ḥanīfs*, who distanced themselves from the Meccan religious system by repudiating the old gods but embracing neither Judaism nor Christianity. Eventually in Mecca and elsewhere a few individuals came to envision the possibility of effecting supra-tribal association through a leadership role common to the confessional religions, that is, prophethood or messengership. The only such individual who succeeded in effecting broad social changes was a member of the Hāshim (Hāshem) clan of Quraysh named Muḥammad ibn ʿAbd Allāh ibn ʿAbd al-Muṭṭalib. One of their own, he accomplished what the Quraysh had started, first by working against them, later by working with them.

MUHAMMAD'S YEARS IN MECCA

When the Prophet Muhammad was born, around 570, the potential for pan-Arab unification seemed nil. However, after he died, in 632, the first generation of his followers were able not only to maintain pan-Arab unification but to expand far beyond the peninsula. Any explanation of such an unprecedented development must include an analysis not only of Muhammad's individual genius but also of his ability to articulate an ideology capable of appealing to multiple constituencies. His approach to the role of prophet allowed a variety of groups to conceptualize and form a single community.

SPIRITUAL AWAKENING

Muhammad was, according to many students of social behaviour, particularly well placed to lead such a social movement; in both ascribed and acquired characteristics he was unusual. Although he was a member of a high-status tribe, he belonged to one of its less well-placed clans. He was fatherless at birth; his mother and grandfather died when he was young, leaving him under the protection of an uncle. Although he possessed certain admirable personality traits to an unusual degree, his commercial success derived not from his own status but from his marriage to a much older woman, a wealthy widow named Khadījah. During the years of his marriage, his personal habits grew increasingly atypical; he began to absent himself in the hills outside Mecca to engage in the solitary spiritual activity of the *ḥanīfs*. At age 40, while on retreat, he saw a figure, whom he later identified as the angel Gabriel, who asked him to "recite" (*iqra'*), then overwhelmed him with a very strong embrace. Muhammad told the stranger that he was not a reciter. But the angel repeated his demand and embrace three times before the verses

The archangel Gabriel is illustrated in the 14th-century manuscript *Jāmiʿ al-tawārīkh* ("Collector of Chronicles") by the Persian historian Rashīd al-Dīn.

of the Qur᾽ān, beginning with "Recite in the Name of thy Lord, who created," were revealed. Although a few individuals, including his wife Khadījah, recognized his experience as that of a messenger of God, the contemporary religious life of most of the Meccans and the surrounding Arabs did not prepare them to share in this recognition easily.

Arabs did recognize several other types of intermediaries with the sacred. Some of the kings of the Yemen are said to have had priestly functions. Tribal leaders, sheikhs, in protecting their tribes' hallowed custom (sunnah), had a spiritual dimension. Tribal Arabs also had their *kāhins*, religious specialists who delivered oracles in ecstatic rhymed prose (*saj*ʿ) and read omens. And they also had their *shāʿirs*, professionally trained oral poets who defended the group's honour, expressed its identity, and engaged in verbal duels with the poets of other groups. The power of the recited word was well established; the poets' words were even likened to arrows that could wound the unprotected enemy. Because Muhammad's utterances seemed similar, at least in form, to those of the *kāhins*, many of his hearers naturally assumed that he was one of the figures with whom they were more familiar. Indeed, Muhammad might not even have attracted attention had he not sounded like other holy men, but, by eschewing any source other than the one supreme being, whom he identified as Allāh ("God") and whose message he regarded as cosmically significant and binding, he was gradually able to distinguish himself from all other intermediaries. Like many successful leaders, Muhammad broke through existing restraints by what might be called transformative conservatism. By combining familiar leadership roles with a less familiar one, he expanded his authority; by giving existing practices a new history, he reoriented them; by assigning a new cause to existing problems, he resolved them. His personal characteristics fit his historical circumstances perfectly.

PUBLIC RECITATIONS

Muhammad's first vision was followed by a brief lull, after which he began to hear messages frequently, entering a special physical state to receive them and returning to normalcy to deliver them orally. Soon he began publicly to recite warnings of an imminent reckoning by Allāh that disturbed the Meccan leaders. Muhammad was one of their own, a man respected for his personal qualities. Yet weakening kinship ties and increasing social diversity were helping him attract followers from many different clans and also from among tribeless persons, giving all of them a new and potentially disruptive affiliation. The fundamentals of his message, delivered often in the vicinity of the Kaʿbah itself, questioned the very reasons for which so many people gathered there. If visitors to the Kaʿbah assumed, as so many Arabs did, that the deities represented by its idols were all useful and accessible in that place, Muhammad spoke, as had Axial Age figures before, of a placeless and timeless deity that not only had created human beings, making them dependent on him, but would also bring them to account at an apocalypse of his own making. In place of time or chance, which the Arabs assumed to govern their destiny, Muhammad installed a final reward or punishment based on individual actions. Such individual accountability to an unseen power that took no account whatsoever of kin relationships and operated beyond the Meccan system could, if taken seriously, undermine any authority the Quraysh had acquired. Muhammad's insistence on the protection of the weak, which echoed Bedouin values, threatened the unbridled amassing of wealth so important to the Meccan oligarchy.

Efforts to Reform Meccan Society

Yet Muhammad also appealed to the town dweller by describing the human being as a member of a polis (city-state) and by suggesting ways to overcome the inequities that such an environment breeds. By insisting that an event of cosmic significance was occurring in Mecca, he made the town the rival of all the greater cities with which

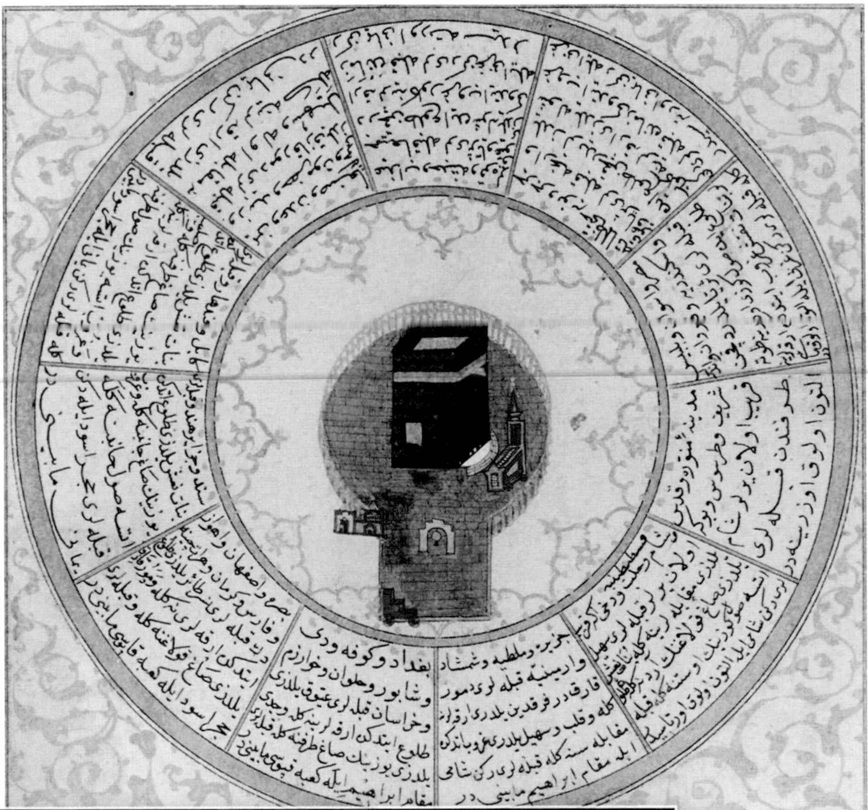

The Ka'bah is illustrated in a 13th-century Arabic manuscript. A pre-Islamic holy site, Muhammad often delivered his recitations near the holy shrine.

the Meccans traded. To Meccans who believed that what went on in their town and at their shrine was hallowed by tribal custom, sunnah, Muhammad replied that their activities in fact were a corrupt form of a practice that had a very long history with the God of whom he spoke. In Muhammad's view, the Kaʿbah had been dedicated to the aniconic worship of the one God (Allāh) by Abraham, who fathered the ancestor of the Israelites, Isḥāq (Isaac), as well as the ancestor of the Arabs, Ismāʿīl (Ishmael). Muhammad asked his hearers not to embrace something new but to abandon the traditional in favour of the original. He appealed to his fellow Quraysh not to reject the sunnah of their ancestors but rather to appreciate and fulfill its true nature. God should be worshipped not through offerings but through prayer and recitation of his messages, and his house should be emptied of its useless idols.

In their initial rejection of his appeal, Muhammad's Meccan opponents took the first step toward accepting the new idea: they attacked it. For it was their rejection of him, as well as his subsequent rejection by many Jews and Christians, that helped to forge Muhammad's followers into a community with an identity of its own and capable of ultimately incorporating its opponents. Muhammad's disparate following was exceptionally vulnerable, bound together not by kinship ties but by a "generic" monotheism that involved being faithful (*muʾmin*) to the message God was sending through their leader. Their vulnerability was mitigated by the absence of formal municipal discipline, but their opponents within the Quraysh could apply informal pressures ranging from harassment and violence against the weakest to a boycott against Muhammad's clan, members of which were persuaded by his uncle Abū Ṭālib to remain loyal even though most of them were not his followers. Meanwhile, Muhammad and his closest associates were thinking about reconstituting themselves as a separate community in a less hostile environment. About 615 some 80 of his followers made an emigration (Hijrah) to Abyssinia, perhaps assuming that they would be welcome in a place that had a history of hostility to the Meccan oligarchy and that worshipped the same God who had sent Muhammad to them, but they eventually returned without establishing a permanent community. During the next decade, continued rejection intensified the group's identity and its search for another home. Although the boycott against Muhammad's clan began to disintegrate, the deaths of his wife and his uncle, about 619, removed an important source of psychological and social support. Muhammad had already begun to preach and attract followers at market gatherings outside Mecca; now he intensified his search for a more hospitable environment. In 620 he met with a delegation of followers from Yathrib, an oasis about 200 miles (320 km) to the northeast; in the next two years their support grew into an offer of protection.

Muhammad's Emigration to Yathrib (Medina)

Like Mecca, Yathrib was experiencing demographic problems: several tribal groups coexisted, descendants of its Arab Jewish founders as well as a number of pagan Arab immigrants divided into two tribes, the Aws and the Khazraj. Unable to resolve their conflicts, the Yathribis invited Muhammad to perform the well-established role of neutral outside arbiter (*ḥakam*). In September 622, having discreetly sent his followers ahead, he and one companion, Abū Bakr, completed the community's second and final emigration, barely avoiding Quraysh attempts to prevent his departure by force. By the time of the emigration, a new label had begun to appear in Muhammad's recitations to describe his followers: in addition to being described in terms of their faithfulness (*īmān*) to God and his messenger, they were also described in terms of their undivided attention—that is, as *muslims*, individuals who assumed the right relationship to God by surrendering (*islām*) to his will. Although the designation *muslim*, derived from *islām*, eventually became a proper name for a specific historical community, at this point it appears to have expressed commonality with other monotheists: like the others, *muslims* faced Jerusalem to pray; Muhammad was believed to have been transported from Jerusalem to the heavens to talk with God; and Abraham, Noah, Moses, David, and Jesus, as well as Muhammad, all were considered to be prophets (*nabīs*) and messengers of the same God. In Yathrib, however, conflicts between other monotheists and the *muslims* sharpened their distinctiveness.

The Forging of Muhammad's Community

As an autonomous community, *muslims* might have become a tribal unit like those with whom they had affiliated, especially because the terms of their immigration gave them no special status. Yet under Muhammad's leadership they developed a social organization that could absorb or challenge everyone around them. They became Muhammad's *ummah* ("community") because they had recognized and supported God's emissary (*rasūl Allāh*). The *ummah's* members differed from one another not by wealth or genealogical superiority but by the degree of their faith and piety, and membership in the community was itself an expression of faith. Anyone could join, regardless of origin, by following Muhammad's lead, and the nature of members' support could vary. In the concept of *ummah*, Muhammad supplied the missing ingredient in the Meccan system: a powerful abstract principle for defining, justifying, and stimulating membership in a single community.

Muhammad made the concept of *ummah* work by expanding his role as arbiter so as to become the sole spokesman for all residents of

It was in Medina that Muhammad forged a community, or *ummah*, of *muslims*, the followers of his recitations. Today Medina is the second-holiest city in Islam.

Yathrib, also known as Medina. Even though the agreement under which Muhammad had emigrated did not obligate non-Muslims to follow him except in his arbitration, they necessarily became involved in the fortunes of his community. By protecting him from his Meccan enemies, the residents of Medina identified with his fate. Those who supported him as Muslims received special designations: the Medinans were called *anṣār* ("helpers"), and his fellow emigrants were distinguished as *muhājirūn* ("emigrants"). He was often able to use revelation to arbitrate.

Because the terms of his emigration did not provide adequate financial support, he began to provide for his community through caravan raiding, a tactic familiar to tribal Arabs. By thus inviting hostility, he required all the Medinans to take sides. Initial failure was followed by success, first at Nakhlah, where the Muslims defied

Meccan custom by violating one of the truce months so essential to Meccan prosperity and prestige. Their most memorable victory occurred in 624 at Badr, against a large Meccan force; they continued to succeed, with only one serious setback, at Uḥud in 625. From that time on, "conversion" to Islam involved joining an established polity, the successes of which were tied to its proper spiritual orientation, regardless of whether the convert shared that orientation completely. During the early years in Medina a major motif of Islamic history emerged: the connection between material success and divine favour, which had also been prominent in the history of the Israelites.

THE UMMAH'S ALLIES AND ENEMIES

During these years, Muhammad used his outstanding knowledge of tribal relations to act as a great tribal leader, or sheikh, further expanding his authority beyond the role that the Medinans had given him. He developed a network of alliances between his *ummah* and neighbouring tribes, and so competed with the Meccans at their own game. He managed and distributed the booty from raiding, keeping one-fifth for the *ummah's* overall needs and distributing the rest among its members. In return, members gave a portion of their wealth as *zakāt*, to help the needy and to demonstrate their awareness of their dependence on God for all of their material benefits. Like other sheikhs, Muhammad contracted numerous, often strategically motivated, marriage alliances. He was also more able to harass and discipline Medinans, Muslim and non-Muslim alike, who did not support his activities fully; he agitated in particular against the Jews, one of whose clans, the Banū Qaynuqāʿ, he expelled.

Increasingly estranged from nonresponsive Jews and Christians, he reoriented his followers' direction of prayer from Jerusalem to Mecca.

Muslim pilgrims visit Mecca, Saudi Arabia, in an illustration from a copy of the Qurʾān. Muhammad instituted the *hajj*, or pilgrimage, to Mecca in his lifetime.

He formally instituted the hajj to Mecca and fasting during the month of Ramadan as distinctive cultic acts, in recognition of the fact that *islām*, a generic act of surrender to God, had become Islam, a proper-name identity distinguished not only from paganism but from other forms of monotheism as well. As more and more of Medina was absorbed into the Muslim community and as the Meccans weakened, Muhammad's authority expanded. He continued to lead a three-pronged campaign—against nonsupporters in Medina, against the Quraysh in Mecca, and against surrounding tribes—and he even ordered raids into southern Syria. Eventually Muhammad became powerful enough to punish nonsupporters severely, especially those who leaned toward Mecca. For example, he had the men of the Qurayẓah clan of Jews in Medina executed after they failed to help him against the Meccan forces at the Battle of the Ditch in 627. But he also used force and diplomacy to bring in other Jewish and Christian groups. Because they were seen, unlike pagans, to have formed *ummahs* of their own around a revelation from God, Jews and Christians were entitled to pay for protection (*dhimmah*). Muhammad thus set a precedent for another major characteristic of Islamicate civilization, that of qualified religious pluralism under Muslim authority.

MUHAMMAD'S LATER RECITATIONS

During these years of warfare and consolidation, Muhammad continued to transmit revealed recitations, though their nature began to change. Some commented on Muhammad's situation, consoled and encouraged his community, explained the continuing resistance of the Meccans, and urged appropriate responses. Some told stories about figures familiar to Jews and Christians but cast in an Islamic framework. Though still delivered in the form of God's direct speech, the messages became longer and less ecstatic, less urgent in their warnings if more earnest in their guidance. Eventually they focused on interpersonal regulations in areas of particular importance for a new community, such as sexuality, marriage, divorce, and inheritance. By this time certain Muslims had begun to write down what Muhammad uttered or to recite passages for worship (*ṣalāt*) and private devotion. The recited word, so important among the Arab tribes, had found a greatly enlarged significance. A competitor for Muhammad's status as God's messenger even declared himself among a nonmember tribe; he was Musaylimah of Yamāmah, who claimed to convey revelations from God. He managed to attract numerous Bedouin Arabs but failed to speak as successfully as Muhammad to the various available constituencies.

Activism in the name of God, both nonmilitary as well as military, would become a permanent strand in Muslim piety. Given the environment in which Muhammad operated, his *ummah* was unlikely to survive without it; to compete as leader of a community, he needed to exhibit military prowess. (Like most successful leaders, however, Muhammad was a moderate and a compromiser; some of his followers were more militant and aggressive than he, and some were less so.) In addition, circumstantial necessity had ideological ramifications. Because Muhammad as messenger was also, by divine providence, leader of an established community, he could easily define the whole realm of social action as an expression of faith. Thus, Muslims were able to identify messengership with worldly leadership to an extent almost unparalleled in the history of religion. There had been activist prophets before Muhammad and there were activist prophets after him, but in no other religious tradition does the image of the activist prophet, and by extension the activist follower, have such a comprehensive and coherent justification in the formative period.

Islam at Muhammad's Death

Muhammad's continuing success gradually impinged on the Quraysh in Mecca. Some defected and joined his community. His marriage to a

Quraysh woman provided him with a useful go-between. In 628 he and his followers tried to make an Islamized hajj but were forestalled by the Meccans. At Al-Ḥudaybiyah, outside Mecca, Muhammad granted a 10-year truce on the condition that the Meccans would allow a Muslim pilgrimage the next year. Even at this point, however, Muhammad's control over his followers had its limits; his more zealous followers agreed to the pact only after much persuasion. As in all instances of charismatic leadership, persisting loyalty was correlated with continuing success. In the next year the Meccans allowed a Muslim hajj; and in the next, 630, the Muslims occupied Mecca without a struggle. Muhammad began to receive deputations from many parts of Arabia. By his death in 632 he was ruler of virtually all of it.

The Meccan Quraysh were allowed to become Muslims without shame. In fact, they quickly became assimilated to the actual *muhājirūn*, even though they had not emigrated to Yathrib themselves. Ironically, in defeat they had accomplished much more than they would have had they achieved victory: the centralization of all of Arabia around their polity and their shrine, the Kaʿbah, which had been emptied of its idols to be filled with an infinitely greater invisible power.

Because intergroup conflict was banned to all members of the *ummah* on the basis of their shared loyalty to the emissary of a single higher authority, the limitations of the Meccan concept of *ḥaram*, according to which the city quarterly became a safe haven, could be overcome. The broader solidarity that Muhammad had begun to build was stabilized only after his death, and this was achieved, paradoxically, by some of the same people who had initially opposed him. In the next two years one of his most significant legacies became apparent: the willingness and ability of his closest supporters to sustain the ideal and the reality of one Muslim community under one leader, even in the face of significant opposition. When Muhammad died, two vital sources of his authority ended—ongoing revelation and his unique ability to exemplify his messages on a daily basis. A leader

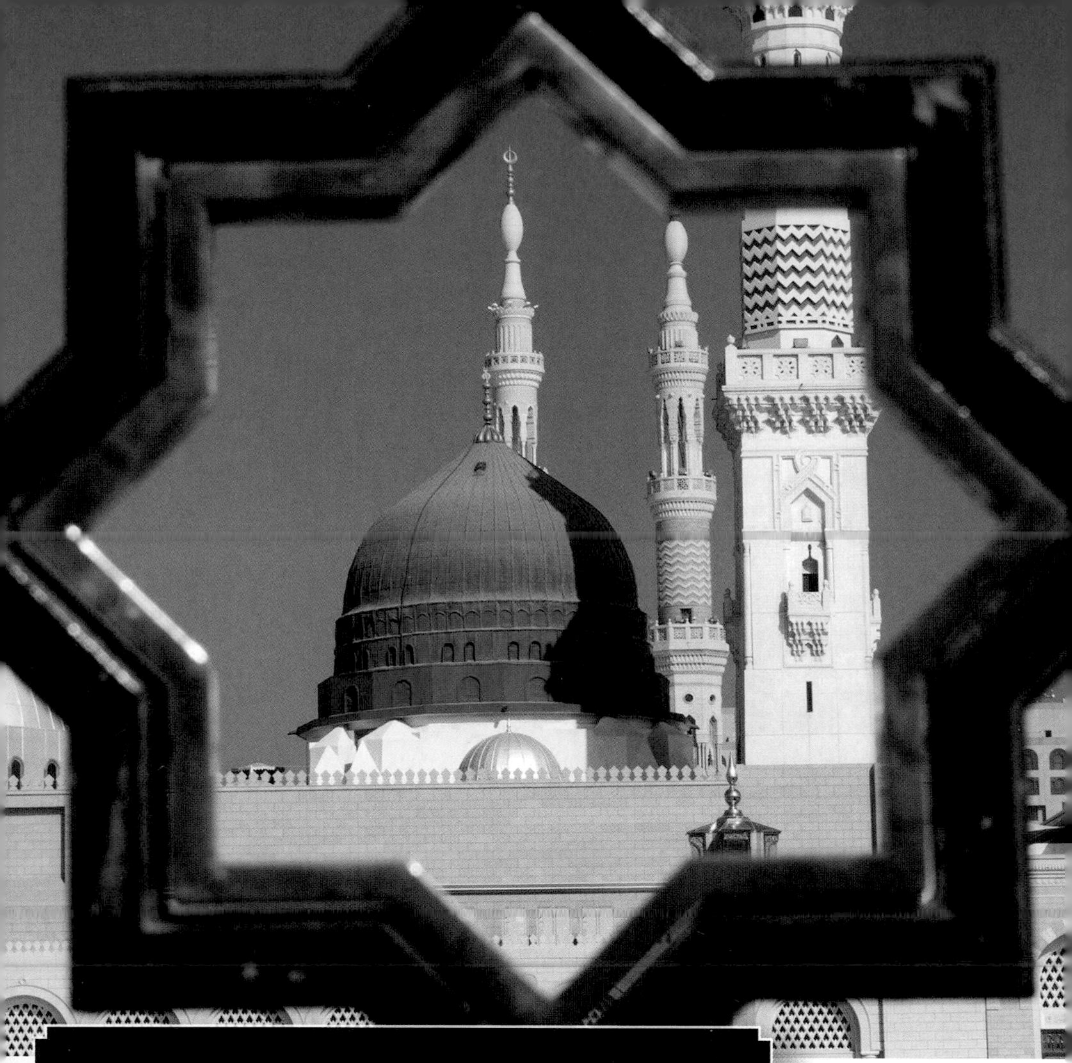

Muhammad's tomb rests within the Prophet's Mosque in Medina. By his death in 632, Muhammad was ruler of virtually all of Arabia.

capable of keeping revelation alive might have had the best chance of inheriting his movement, but no Muslim claimed messengership, nor had Muhammad unequivocally designated any other type of successor. The *anṣār*, his early supporters in Medina, moved to elect their own leader, leaving the *muhājirūn* to choose theirs, but a small number of muhājirūn managed to impose one of their own over the whole. That man was Abū Bakr, one of Muhammad's earliest followers and the

CALIPH

The caliph (in Arabic: *khalīfah*, "successor") is ruler of the Muslim community. When the Prophet Muhammad died (June 8, 632 CE), Abū Bakr succeeded to his political and administrative functions as *khalīfah rasūl Allāh*, "successor of the Messenger of God," but it was probably under ʿUmar ibn al-Khaṭṭāb, the second *caliph*, that the term caliph came into use as a title of the civil and religious head of the Muslim state. In the same sense, the term was employed in the Qurʾān in reference both to Adam and to David as the vice-regents of God.

Abū Bakr and his three immediate successors are known as the "perfect" or "rightly guided" caliphs (*al-khulafāʾ al-rāshidun*). After them the title was borne by the 14 Umayyad caliphs of Damascus and subsequently by the 38 ʿAbbāsid caliphs of Baghdad, whose dynasty fell before the Mongols in 1258. There were titular caliphs of ʿAbbāsid descent in Cairo under the Mamlūks from 1258 until 1517, when the last caliph was captured by the Ottoman sultan Selim I. The Ottoman sultans then claimed the title and used it until it was abolished by the Turkish Republic on March 3, 1924.

After the fall of the Umayyad dynasty at Damascus (750), the title of caliph was also assumed by the Spanish branch of the family who ruled in Spain at Córdoba (755–1031), and it was also assumed by the Fāṭimid rulers of Egypt (909–1171), who claimed to descend from Fāṭimah (daughter of Muhammad) and her husband, ʿAli.

According to the Shīʿites, who call the supreme office the "imamate," or leadership, no caliph is legitimate unless he is a lineal descendant of the Prophet Muhammad. The Sunnis insist that the office belongs to the tribe of Quraysh, to which Muhammad himself belonged, but this condition would have disallowed the claim of the Turkish sultans, who held the office after the last ʿAbbāsid caliph of Cairo transferred it to Selim I.

father of his favourite wife, ʿĀʾishah. The title Abū Bakr took, *khalīfah* (caliph), meaning deputy or successor, echoed revealed references to those who assist major leaders and even God himself. To *khalīfah* he appended *rasūl Allāh*, so that his authority was based on his assistance to Muhammad as messenger of God.

ABŪ BAKR'S SUCCESSION

Abū Bakr soon confronted two new threats: the secession of many of the tribes that had joined the *ummah* after 630 and the appearance among them of other prophet figures who claimed continuing guidance from God. In withdrawing, the tribes appear to have been able to distinguish loyalty to Muhammad from full acceptance of the uniqueness and permanence of his message. The appearance of other prophets illustrates a general phenomenon in the history of religion: the volatility of revelation as a source of authority. When successfully claimed, it has almost no competitor; once opened, it is difficult to close; and, if it cannot be contained and focused at the appropriate moment, its power disperses. Jews and Christians had responded to this dilemma in their own ways; now it was the turn of the Muslims, whose future was dramatically affected by Abū Bakr's response. He put an end to revelation with a combination of military force and coherent rhetoric. He defined withdrawal from Muhammad's coalition as ingratitude to or denial of God (the concept of *kufr*); thus he gave secession (*riddah*) cosmic significance as an act of apostasy punishable, according to God's revealed messages to Muhammad, by death. He declared that the secessionists had become Muslims, and thus servants of God, by joining Muhammad; they were not free not to be Muslims, nor could they be Muslims, and thus loyal to God, under any leader whose legitimacy did not derive from Muhammad.

Finally, he declared Muhammad to be the last prophet God would send, relying on a reference to Muhammad in one of the revealed messages as *khatm al-anbiyā'* ("seal of the prophets"). In his ability to interpret the events of his reign from the perspective of Islam, Abū Bakr demonstrated the power of the new conceptual vocabulary Muhammad had introduced.

Had Abū Bakr not asserted the independence and uniqueness of Islam, the movement he had inherited could have been splintered or absorbed by other monotheistic communities or by new Islam-like movements led by other tribal figures. Moreover, had he not quickly made the ban on secession and intergroup conflict yield material success, his chances for survival would have been very slim, because Arabia's resources could not support his state. To provide an adequate fiscal base, Abū Bakr enlarged impulses present in pre-Islamic Mecca and in the *ummah*. At his death he was beginning to turn his followers to raiding non-Muslims in the only direction where that was possible, the north. Migration into Syria and Iraq already had a long history; Arabs, both migratory and settled, were already present there. Indeed, some of them were already launching raids when 'Umar I, Abū Bakr's acknowledged successor, assumed the caliphate in 634. The ability of the Medinan state to absorb random action into a relatively centralized movement of expansion testifies to the strength of the new ideological and administrative patterns inherent in the concept of *ummah*.

The fusion of two once separable phenomena, membership in Muhammad's community and faith in Islam—the mundane and the spiritual—would become one of Islam's most distinctive features. Becoming and being Muslim always involved doing more than it involved believing. On balance, Muslims have always favoured orthopraxy (correctness of practice) over orthodoxy (correctness of doctrine). Being Muslim has always meant making a commitment to a set of behavioral patterns because they reflect the right orientation to God. Where choices were later posed, they were posed not in terms of religion and politics, or church and state, but between living in the world the right way or the wrong way. Just as classical Islamicate languages developed no equivalents for the words *religion* and *politics*, modern European languages have developed no adequate terms to capture the choices as Muslims have posed them.

Chapter 3

Conversion and Crystallization (634–870)

The Arab conquests are often viewed as a discrete period. The end of the conquests appears to be a convenient dividing line because it coincides with a conventional watershed, the overthrow of the Umayyad caliphs by the ʿAbbāsids. To illustrate their role in broader social and cultural change, however, the military conquests should be included in a period more than twice as long, during which the conquest of the hearts and minds of the majority of the subject population also occurred.

Social and Cultural Transformations

Between 634 and 870 Islam was transformed from the badge of a small Arab ruling class to the dominant faith of a vast empire that stretched from the western Mediterranean into Central Asia. As a result of this long and gradual period of conversion, Arab cultures intermingled with the indigenous cultures of the conquered peoples to produce Islam's fundamental orientations and identities. The Arabic language became a vehicle for the transmission of high culture, even though the Arabs remained a minority; for the first time in the history of the Nile-to-Oxus region, a new language of high culture, carrying a great cultural florescence, replaced all previous languages of high culture. Trade and taxation replaced

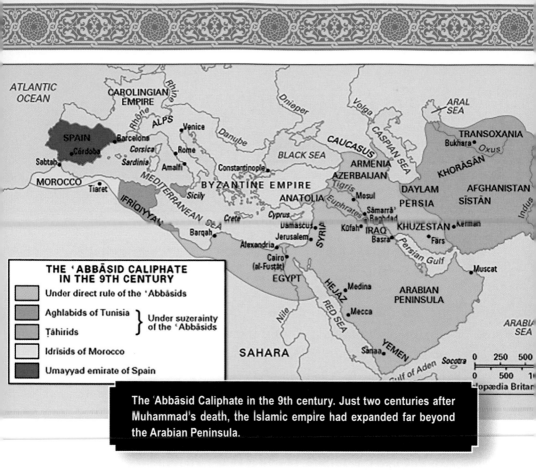

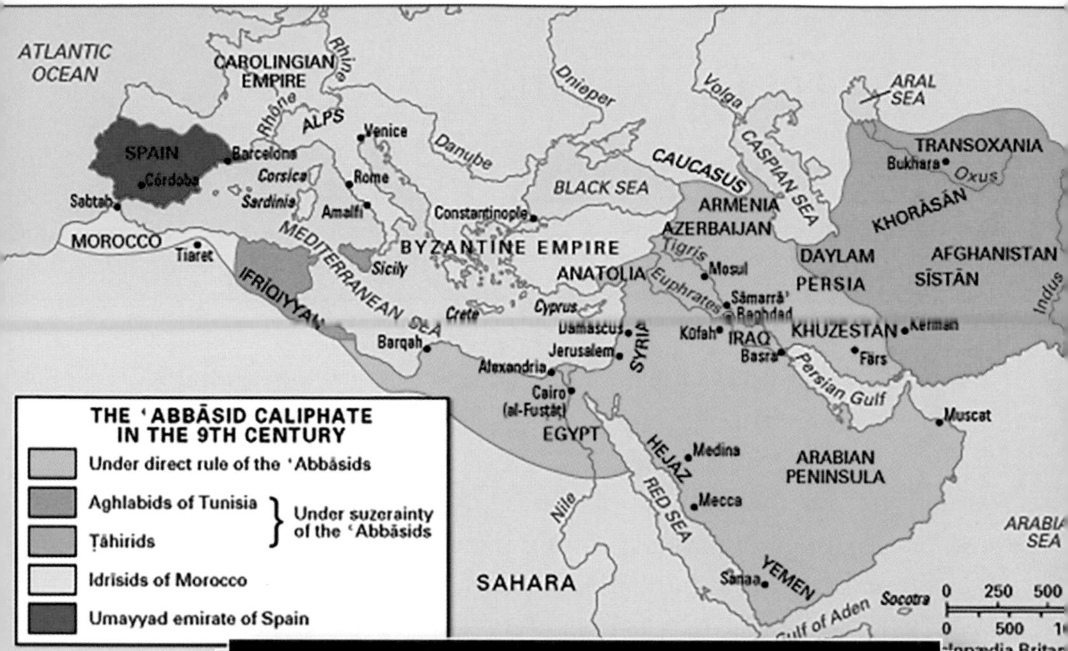

The ʿAbbāsid Caliphate in the 9th century. Just two centuries after Muhammad's death, the Islamic empire had expanded far beyond the Arabian Peninsula.

booty as the fiscal basis of the Muslim state; a nontribal army replaced a tribal one; and a centralized empire became a nominal confederation, with all of the social dislocation and rivalries those changes imply.

Yet despite continuous internal dissension, virtually no Muslim raised the possibility of there being more than one legitimate leader. Furthermore, the impulse toward solidarity, inherited from Muhammad and Abū Bakr, may have actually been encouraged by persisting minority status. While Muslims were a minority, they naturally formed a conception of Islamic dominance as territorial rather than religious, and of unconverted non-Muslim communities as secondary members. In one important respect the Islamic faith differed from all other major religious traditions: the formative period of the faith coincided with its political domination of a rich complex of old cultures. As a result, during the formative period of their civilization, the Muslims could both introduce new elements and reorient old ones in creative ways.

Just as Muhammad fulfilled and redirected ongoing tendencies in Arabia, the builders of early Islamicate civilization carried forth and transformed developments in the Roman and Sāsānian territories in which they first dominated. While Muhammad was emerging as a leader in the Hejaz, the Byzantine and Sāsānian emperors were ruling states that resembled what the Islamicate empire was to become. Byzantine rule stretched from North Africa into Syria and sometimes Iraq; the Sāsānians competed with the Byzantines in Syria and Iraq and extended their sway, at its furthest, across the Oxus River. Among their subjects were speakers and writers of several major languages—various forms of Aramaic, such as Mandaean and Syriac; Greek; Arabic; and Middle Persian. In fact, a significant number of persons were probably bilingual or trilingual. Both the Byzantine and the Sāsānian empire declared an official religion, Christianity and Zoroastrianism, respectively.

The Sāsānian empire in the early 7th century was ruled by a religion-backed centralized monarchy with an elaborate bureaucratic structure that was reproduced on a smaller scale at the provincial courts of its appointed governors. Its religious demography was complex, encompassing Christians of many persuasions, Monophysites, Nestorians, Orthodox, and others; pagans; gnostics; Jews; Zoroastrians. Minority religious communities were becoming more clearly organized and isolated. The population included priests; traders and merchants; landlords (*dihqāns*), sometimes living not on the land but as absentees in the cities; pastoralists; and large numbers of peasant agriculturalists. In southern Iraq, especially in and around towns like Al-Ḥīrah, it included migratory and settled Arabs as well.

Both empires relied on standing armies for their defense and on agriculture, taxation, conquest, and trade for their resources. When the Muslim conquests began, the Byzantines and Sāsānians had been in conflict for a century; in the most recent exchanges, the Sāsānians had established direct rule in al-Ḥīrah, further exposing its many Arabs to their administration. When the Arab conquests began, representatives of Byzantine and Sāsānian rule on Arabia's northern borders were not strong enough to resist.

Shown is a detail of a fresco (painted 1452–1466 by Piero della Francesca) illustrating battle between the Byzantine emperor Heraclius and the Sāsānian king Khosrow II. At the time of the start of the Muslim conquests, the two major regional empires, the Byzantines and the Sāsānians, had been warring for a century.

ʿUmar I's Succession

Abū Bakr's successor in Medina, ʿUmar I (ruled 634–644), had not so much to stimulate conquest as to organize and channel it. He chose as leaders skillful managers experienced in trade and commerce as well as warfare and imbued with an ideology that provided their activities with a cosmic significance. The total numbers involved in the initial conquests may have been relatively small, perhaps fewer than 50,000, divided into numerous shifting groups. Yet few actions took place without any sanction from the Medinan government or one of its appointed commanders. The fighters, or *muqātilah*, could generally accomplish much more with Medina's support than without. ʿUmar, one of Muhammad's earliest and staunchest supporters, had quickly developed an administrative system of manifestly superior effectiveness. He defined the *ummah* as a continually expansive polity managed by a new ruling elite, which included successful military commanders like Khālid ibn al-Walīd. Even after the conquests ended, this sense of expansiveness continued to be expressed in the way Muslims divided the world into their own zone, the Dār al-Islām, and the zone into which they could and should expand, the Dār al-Ḥarb, the abode of war. The norms of ʿUmar's new elite were supplied by Islam as it was then understood. Taken together, Muhammad's revelations from God and his Sunnah (precedent-setting example) defined the cultic and personal practices that distinguished Muslims from others: prayer, fasting, pilgrimage, charity, avoidance of pork and intoxicants, membership in one community centred at Mecca, and activism (jihad) on the community's behalf.

ʿUmar symbolized this conception of the *ummah* in two ways. He assumed an additional title, *amīr al-muʾminīn* ("commander of the faithful"), which linked organized activism with faithfulness (*īmān*), the earliest defining feature of the Muslim. He also adopted a lunar calendar that began with the emigration (Hijrah), the moment at which a group of individual followers of Muhammad had become an active social presence. Because booty was the *ummah's* major resource, ʿUmar concentrated on ways to distribute and sustain it. He established a *dīwān*, or register, to pay all members of the ruling elite and the conquering forces, from Muhammad's family on down, in order of entry into the *ummah*. The immovable booty was kept for the state. After the government's fifth-share of the movable booty was reserved, the rest was distributed according to the *dīwān*. The *muqātilah* he stationed as an occupying army in garrisons (*amṣār*) constructed in locations strategic to further conquest: al-Fusṭāṭ in Egypt, Damascus in Syria, Kūfah and Basra in Iraq. The garrisons attracted indigenous population and initiated significant demographic changes, such as a population shift from northern to southern Iraq. They also inaugurated the rudiments of an "Islamic" daily life; each garrison was commanded by a caliphal appointee, responsible for setting aside an area for prayer, a mosque (*masjid*), named for the prostrations (*sujūd*) that had become a characteristic element in the five daily worship sessions (*ṣalāts*). There the fighters could hear God's revelations to Muhammad recited by men trained in that emerging art. The most pious might commit the whole to memory. There too, the Friday midday *ṣalāt* could be performed communally, accompanied by an important educational device, the sermon (*khuṭbah*), through which the fighters could be instructed in the principles of the faith. The mosque fused the practical and the spiritual in a special way: because the Friday prayer included an expression of loyalty to the ruler, it could also provide an opportunity to declare rebellion.

The series of ongoing conquests that fueled this system had their most extensive phase under ʿUmar and his successor ʿUthmān ibn ʿAffān (ruled 644–656). Within 25 years Muslim Arab forces created the first empire to permanently link western Asia with the Mediterranean. Within another century Muslim conquerors surpassed the achievement of Alexander the Great, not only in the durability of their accomplishment but in its scope as well, reaching from the Iberian Peninsula to Central Asia. Resistance was generally slight and nondestructive, and conquest through capitulation was preferred to conquest by force.

After Sāsānian Al-Ḥīrah fell in 633, a large Byzantine force was defeated in Syria, opening the way to the final conquest of Damascus in 636. The next year further gains were made in Sāsānian territory, especially at the Battle of al-Qādisiyyah, and in the next the focus returned to Syria and the taking of Jerusalem. By 640 Roman control in Syria was over, and by 641 the Sāsānians had lost all their

The ancient city of Persepolis, located near the Sāsānian capital of Istakhr, was one of the final cities to fall during the Muslim conquests.

territory west of the Zagros. During the years 642 to 646 Egypt was taken under the leadership of ʿAmr ibn al-ʿĀṣ, who soon began raids into what the Muslims called the Maghrib, the lands west of Egypt. Shortly thereafter, in the east, Persepolis fell; in 651 the defeat and assassination of the last Sāsānian emperor, Yazdegerd III, marked the end of the 400-year-old Sāsānian empire.

ʿUTHMĀN'S SUCCESSION AND POLICIES

This phase of conquest ended under ʿUthmān and ramified widely. ʿUthmān may even have sent an emissary to China in 651; by the end of the 7th century Arab Muslims were trading there. The fiscal strain of such expansion and the growing independence of local Arabs outside the peninsula underlay the persisting discontents that surfaced toward the end of ʿUthmān's reign. The very way in which he was made caliph had already signaled the potential for competition over leadership and resources. Perceived as pliable and docile, he was the choice of the small committee charged by the dying ʿUmar with selecting one of their own number. Once in office, however, ʿUthmān acted to establish the power of Medina over and against some of the powerful Quraysh families at Mecca and local notables outside Arabia. He was accused of nepotism for relying on his own family, the Banū Umayyah, whose talents ʿUmar had already recognized. Among his many other "objectionable" acts was his call for the production of a single standard collection of Muhammad's messages from God, which was known simply as the Qurʾān ("Recitation" or "Recitations"). Simultaneously he ordered the destruction of any other collections. Although they might have differed only in minor respects, they represented the independence of local communities. Above all, ʿUthmān was the natural target of anyone dissatisfied with the distribution of the conquest's wealth, since he represented and defended a system that defined all income as Medina's to distribute.

The difficulties of ʿUthmān's reign took more than a century to resolve. They were the inevitable result not just of the actions of individuals but of the whole process initiated by Muhammad's achievements. His coalition had been fragile. He had disturbed existing social arrangements without being able to reconstruct and stabilize new ones quickly. Into a society organized along family lines, he had introduced the supremacy of trans-kinship ties. Yet he had been forced to make use of kinship ties himself; and, despite his egalitarian message, he had introduced new inequities by granting privileges to the earliest and most intensely devoted followers of his cause. Furthermore, personal rivalries were stimulated by his charisma; individuals like his wife ʿĀʾishah, his daughter Fāṭimah, and her husband ʿAlī frequently vied for his affection. ʿUmar's *dīwān* had, then, reinforced old inequities by extending privileges to wealthy high-placed Meccans, and it had introduced new tensions by assigning a lower status to those, indigenous or immigrant to the provinces, who joined the cause later (but who felt themselves to be making an equivalent or greater contribution). Other tensions resulted from conditions in the conquered lands: the initial isolation of Arab Muslims, and even Arab Christians who fought with them, from the indigenous non-Arab population; the discouragement of non-Arab converts, except as clients (*mawālī*) of Arab tribes; the administrative dependence of peninsular Arabs on local Arabs and non-Arabs; and the development of a tax system that discriminated against non-Muslims.

The ensuing conflicts were played out in a series of intra-Muslim disputes that began with ʿUthmān's assassination in 656 and continued to the end of the period under discussion. The importance of kinship ties persisted, but they were gradually replaced by the identities of a new social order. These new identities resulted from

Muslim responses to anti-Muslim activity as well as from Muslim participation in a series of controversies focused on the issue of leadership. Because the *ummah*, unified under one leader, was seen as an earthly expression of God's favour, and because God was seen as the controller of all aspects of human existence, the identities formed in the course of the *ummah's* early history could fuse dimensions that secular modern observers are able to distinguish—religious, social, political, and economic. Furthermore, intra-Muslim rivalries changed during the conversion period; the meaningfulness of the new identities expanded as non-Muslims contributed to Islam's formation, through opposition or through conversion, and the key issues broadened as the participating constituencies enlarged. At first the disputes were coterminous with intra-Arab, indeed even intra-Quraysh, rivalries; only later did they involve persons of other backgrounds. Thus the faith of Islam was formed in conjunction with the crises that attended the establishment of rule by Muslims. Muslims might have produced an extremely localized and exclusivistic religion; but in spite of, and perhaps because of, their willingness to engage in continuing internal conflicts, they produced one of the most unified religious traditions in human history.

THE FOUR *FITNAHS*

By the end of the period of conversion and crystallization, Muslim historians would retrospectively identify four discrete periods of conflict and label them *fitnahs*, trials or temptations to test the unity of the ummah. Many historians also came to view some identities formed during the *fitnahs* as authentic and others as deviant. This retrospective interpretation may be anachronistic and misleading. The entire period between 656 and the last quarter of the 9th century was conflict-ridden, and the *fitnahs* merely mark periods of intensification; yet the most striking characteristic of the period was the pursuit of unity.

The First *Fitnah*

In the first two *fitnahs* the claimants to the caliphate relied on their high standing among the Quraysh and their local support in either Arabia, Iraq, or Syria. Competition for the caliphate thus reflected rivalries among the leading Arab families as well as regional interests. The first *fitnah* occurred between ʿUthmān's assassination in 656 and the accession of his kinsman Muʿāwiyah I in 661 and included the caliphate of ʿAlī, the cousin and son-in-law of Muhammad. It involved a three-way contest between ʿAlī's party in Iraq; a coalition of important Quraysh families in Mecca, including Muhammad's wife ʿĀʾishah and Ṭalḥah and Zubayr; and the party of Muʿāwiyah, the governor of Syria and a member of ʿUthmān's clan, the Banū Umayyah. Ostensibly the conflict focused on whether ʿUthmān had been assassinated justly, whether ʿAlī had been involved, and whether ʿUthmān's death should be avenged by Muʿāwiyah or by the leading Meccans.

ʿAlī and his party (*shīʿah*) at first gained power over the representatives of the other leading Meccan families, then lost it permanently to Muʿāwiyah, who elevated Damascus, which had been his provincial capital, to the status of imperial capital. Disappointed at the Battle of Ṣiffīn (657) with ʿAlī's failure to insist on his right to rule, a segment of his partisans withdrew, accordingly calling themselves Khawārij (Khārijites, "Seceders"). Their spiritual heirs would come to recognize any pious Muslim as leader. Meanwhile, another segment of ʿAlī's party intensified their loyalty to him as a just and heroic leader who was one of Muhammad's dearest intimates and the father of his only male descendants.

The Battle of Ṣiffīn (657) ultimately undermined the authority of ʿAlī as fourth caliph and prepared for the establishment of the Umayyad dynasty.

KHĀRIJITES

The Khārijites represent the earliest Islamic sect, tracing their beginning to a religio-political controversy over the Caliphate.

After the indecisive Battle of Ṣiffīn (July 657) between Muhammad's son-in-law and the fourth caliph ʿAlī and the Syrian governor Muʿāwiyah's forces, ʿAlī was forced to agree to arbitration by umpires. This concession aroused the anger of a large group of ʿAlī's followers, who protested that "judgment belongs to God alone" (Qurʾān 6:57) and believed that arbitration would be a rejection of the Qurʾānic dictum "If one party rebels against the other, fight against that which rebels" (49:9). A small number of these followers withdrew (*kharajū*) to the village of Ḥarūrāʾ under the leadership of Ibn Wahb and, when arbitration proved disastrous to ʿAlī, were joined near Nahrawān by a larger group.

The Khārijites were opposed equally to ʿAlī's claims and to those of Muʿāwiyah. They rejected not only the existing caliphal candidates but all Muslims who did not accept their views, and the Khārijites engaged in campaigns of harassment and terror.

The Khārijites' harassment of various Muslim governments was less a matter of personal enmity than a practical exercise of their religious beliefs. They held that the judgment of God could only be expressed through the free choice of the entire Muslim community. They insisted that anyone, even a black slave, could be elected caliph if he possessed the necessary qualifications, chiefly religious piety and moral purity. A caliph may be deposed upon the commission of any major sin. The Khārijites thus set themselves against the legitimist claims (to the Caliphate) of the tribe of Quraysh (among the Sunnites) and of ʿAlī's descendants (among the Shīʿites). As proponents of the democratic principle, the Khārijites drew to themselves many who were dissatisfied with the existing political and religious authorities.

continued on the next page

continued from the previous page

Besides their democratic theory of the Caliphate, the Khārijites were known for their puritanism and fanaticism. Any Muslim who committed a major sin was considered an apostate. Luxury, music, games, and having concubines without the consent of wives were forbidden. Intermarriage and relations with other Muslims were strongly discouraged. The doctrine of justification by faith without works was rejected, and literal interpretation of the Qur'ān was insisted upon.

Within the Khārijite movement the Azāriqah of Basra were the most extreme subsect, separating themselves from the Muslim community and declaring death to all sinners and their families. The more moderate subsect of the Ibāḍīyah, however, survived into the 20th century in North Africa, Oman, and Zanzibar, with about 500,000 members.

THE SECOND *FITNAH*

The second *fitnah* followed Muʿāwiyah's caliphate (661–680), which itself was not free from strife, and coincided with the caliphates of Muʿāwiyah's son Yazīd I (ruled 680–683), whom he designated as successor, and Yazīd's three successors. This *fitnah* was a second-generation reprise of the first; some of the personnel of the former were descendants or relatives of the leaders of the latter. Once again, different regions supported different claimants, as new tribal divisions emerged in the garrison towns; and once again, representatives of the Syrian Umayyads prevailed. In 680, at Karbalāʾ in Iraq, Yazīd's army murdered al-Ḥusayn, a son of ʿAlī and grandson of Muhammad, along with a small group of supporters, accusing them of rebellion; and even though the Umayyads subdued Iraq, rebellions in the name of this or that relative of ʿAlī continued, attracting more and more non-Arab

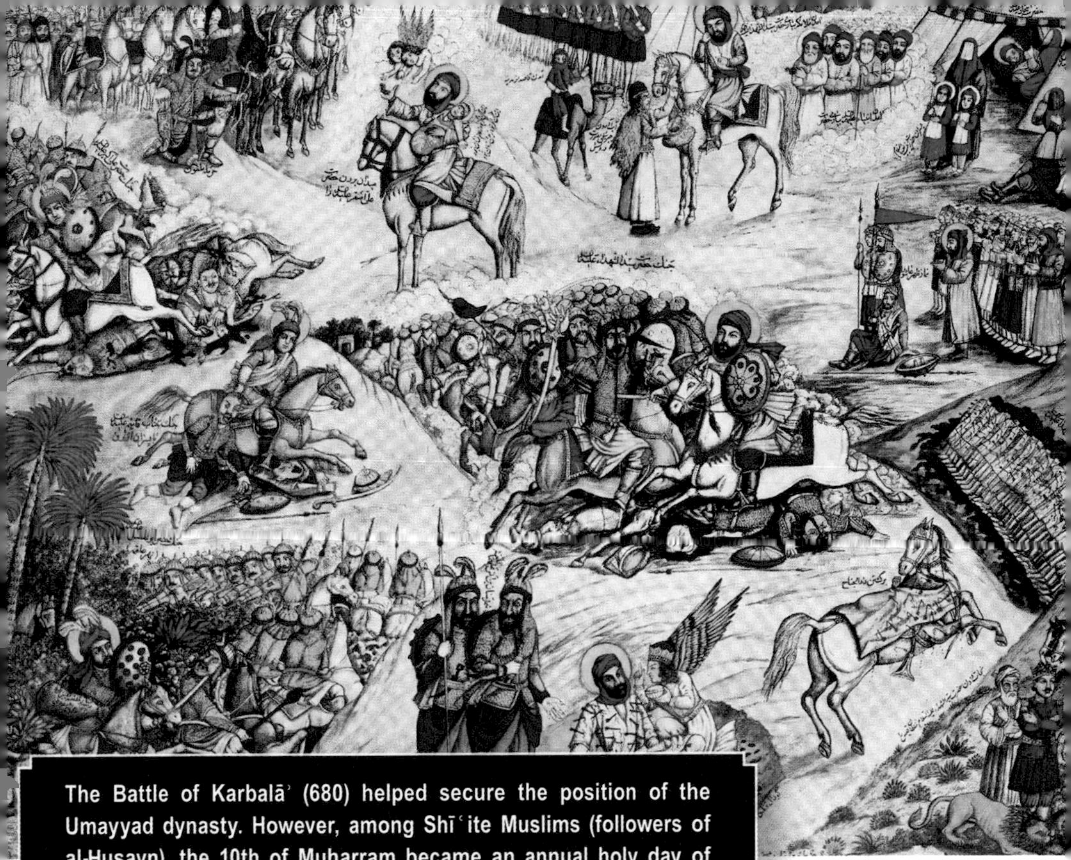

The Battle of Karbalāʾ (680) helped secure the position of the Umayyad dynasty. However, among Shīʿite Muslims (followers of al-Ḥusayn), the 10th of Muharram became an annual holy day of public mourning over al-Ḥusayn's death.

support and introducing new dimensions to his cause. In the Hejaz the Marwānid branch of the Umayyads, descendants of Marwān I who claimed the caliphate in 684, fought against ʿAbd Allāh ibn al-Zubayr for years; by the time they defeated him, they had lost most of Arabia to Kharijite rebels.

During the period of the first two *fitnahs*, resistance to Muslim rule was an added source of conflict. Some of this resistance took the form of syncretic or anti-Islamic religious movements. For example, during the second *fitnah*, in Iraq a Jew named Abū ʿĪsā al-ʿIṣfahānī led a syncretic movement (that is, a movement combining different forms of belief or practice) on the basis of his claim to be a prophet (an option not generally open to Muslim rebels) and forerunner of the messiah. He viewed Muhammad and Jesus as messengers sent not to all humanity but only to their own communities, so he urged each community to continue in its own tradition as he helped prepare for the coming of the messiah. In other areas, such as the newly conquered Maghrib, resistance took the form of large-scale military hostility. In the 660s the Umayyads had expanded their conflict with the Byzantine Empire by competing for bases in coastal North Africa; it soon became clear, however, that only a full-fledged occupation would serve their purposes. That occupation was begun by ʿUqbah ibn Nāfiʿ, the founder of al-Qayrawān (Kairouan, in modern Tunisia) and, as Sīdī (Saint) ʿUqbah, the first of many Maghribi Muslim saints. It eventually resulted in the incorporation of large numbers of pagan or Christianized Amazigh (plural: Imazighen; Berber) tribes, the first large-scale forcible incorporation of tribal peoples since the secession of tribes under Abū Bakr. But first the Arab armies met fierce resistance from two individuals—one a man, Kusaylah, and one a woman, al-Kāhinah—who became Amazigh heroes. Amazigh resistance was not controlled until the end of the 7th century, after which the Imazighen participated in the further conquest of the Maghrib and the Iberian Peninsula.

The Emergent Islamic Civilization

During the caliphate of ʿAbd al-Malik ibn Marwān (ruled 685–705), which followed the end of the second *fitnah*, and under his successors during the next four decades, the problematic consequences of the conquests became much more visible. Like their Byzantine and late Sāsānian predecessors, the Marwānid caliphs nominally ruled the various religious communities but allowed the communities' own appointed or elected officials to administer most internal affairs. Yet now the right of religious communities to live in this fashion was justified by the Qurʾān and the Sunnah; as peoples with revealed books *(ahl al-kitāb)*, they deserved protection (*dhimmah*) in return for a payment. The Arabs also formed a single religious community whose right to rule over the non-Arab protected communities the Marwānids sought to maintain.

To signify this supremacy, as well as his co-optation of previous legitimacy, ʿAbd al-Malik ordered the construction of the monumental Dome of the Rock in Jerusalem, a major centre of non-Muslim population. The site chosen was sacred to Jews and Christians because of its associations with biblical history; it later gained added meaning for Muslims, who believed it to be the starting point for Muhammad's *miʿrāj* (midnight journey to heaven). Although the Dome of the Rock

The construction of the Dome of the Rock in Jerusalem symbolized the expansion of Muslim rule over regions with predominantly non-Muslim populations. The site chosen for the mosque was sacred to both Jews and Christians because of biblical associations.

(whose original function remains unclear) and many early mosques resembled contemporary Christian churches, gradually an Islamic aesthetic emerged: a dome on a geometrical base, accompanied by a minaret from which to deliver the call to prayer, and an emphasis on surface decoration that combined arabesque and geometrical design with calligraphic representations of God's Word. ʿAbd al-Malik took other steps to mark the distinctiveness of Islamic rule: for example, he encouraged the use of Arabic as the language of government and had Islamized coins minted to replace the Byzantine and Sāsānian-style coinage that had continued to be used since the conquests. During the Marwānid period the Muslim community was further consolidated by the regularization of the public cult and the crystallization of a set of five minimal duties (sometimes called pillars).

Yet the Marwānids also depended heavily on the help of non-Arab administrative personnel (*kuttāb*, singular *kātib*) and on administrative practices (e.g., a set of government bureaus) inherited from Byzantine and, in particular, late Sāsānian practice. Pre-Islamic writings on governance translated into Arabic, especially from Middle Persian, influenced caliphal style. The governing structure at Damascus and in the provinces began to resemble pre-Islamic monarchy, and thus appealed to a majority of subjects, whose heritage extolled the absolute authority of a divinely sanctioned ruler. Much of the inspiration for this development came from ʿAbd al-Malik's administrator in the eastern territories, al-Ḥajjāj ibn Yūsuf al-Thaqafī, who was himself an admirer of Sāsānian practice.

The Marwānid caliphs, as rulers of Muslims and non-Muslims alike, had thus been forced to respond to a variety of expectations. Ironically, it was their defense of the importance and distinctiveness of the Arabic language and the Islamic community, not their responsiveness to non-Muslim preferences, that prepared the way for the gradual incorporation of most of the subject population into the *ummah*. As the conquests slowed and the isolation of the fighters (*muqātilah*) became less necessary, it became more and more difficult to keep Arabs garrisoned. The sedentarization of Arabs that had begun in the Hejaz was being repeated and extended outside the peninsula. As the tribal links that had so dominated Umayyad politics began to break down, the meaningfulness of tying non-Arab converts to Arab tribes as clients was diluted; moreover, the number of non-Muslims who wished to join the *ummah* was already becoming too large for this process to work effectively.

Simultaneously, the growing prestige and elaboration of things Arabic and Islamic made them more attractive to non-Arab Muslims and to non-Muslims alike. The more the Muslim rulers succeeded, the more prestige their customs, norms, and habits acquired. Heirs to the considerable agricultural and commercial resources of the Nile-to-Oxus region, they increased its prosperity and widened its horizons by extending its control far to the east and west. Arabic, which occasionally had been used for administrative purposes in earlier empires, now became a valuable lingua franca. As Muslims continued to adapt to rapidly changing circumstances, they needed Arabic to reflect upon and elaborate what they had inherited from the Hejaz. Because the Qur᾽ān, translation of which was prohibited, was written in a form of Arabic that quickly became archaic to Muslims living in the garrisons and because it contained references to life in Arabia before and during Muhammad's time, full understanding of the text required special effort. Scholars began to study the religion and poetry of the *jāhiliyyah*, the times of ignorance before God's revelation to Muhammad. Philologians soon emerged, in the Hejaz as well as in the garrisons. Many Muslims cultivated reports, which came to be known as Hadith, of what Muhammad had said and done, in order to develop a clearer and fuller picture of his Sunnah. These materials were sometimes gathered into accounts of his campaigns, called *maghāzī*. The emulation of Muhammad's Sunnah was a major factor in the development of recognizably "Muslim" styles of personal piety and public decision-making. As differences in the garrisons needed to be settled according to "Islamic" principles, the caliphs appointed arbitrating judges, *qāḍīs*, who were knowledgeable in the Qurʾān and the Sunnah. The pursuit of legal knowledge, *fiqh*, was taken up in many locales and informed by local pre-Islamic custom and Islamic resources. These special forms of knowledge began to be known as *ʿulūm* (singular *ʿilm*) and the persons who pursued them as *ulama* (*ʿulamaʾ*, singular *ʿalim*), a role that provided new sources of prestige and influence, especially for recent converts or sons of converts.

Muslims outside Arabia were also affected by interacting with members of the religious communities over which they ruled. When protected non-Muslims converted, they brought new expectations and habits with them; Islamic eschatology is one area that reflects such enrichment. Unconverted protected groups (*dhimmīs*) were equally influential. Expressions of Islamic identity often had to take into account the critique of non-Muslims, just as the various non-Muslim traditions were affected by contact with Muslims. This interaction had special consequences in the areas of prophethood and revelation, where major shifts and accommodations occurred among Jews, Christians, Zoroastrians, and Muslims during the first two centuries of their coexistence. Muslims attempted to establish Muhammad's legitimacy as an heir to Jewish and Christian prophethood, while non-Muslims tried to distinguish their prophets and scriptures from Muhammad and the Qurʾān. Within the emergent Islamicate civilization, the separate religious communities continued to go their own way, but the influence of Muslim rule and the intervention of the caliphs in their internal affairs could not help but affect them. The Babylonian Talmud, completed during these years, bears traces of early interaction among communities. In Iraq caliphal policy helped promote the Jewish gaons (local rabbinic authorities) over the exilarch (a central secular leader). Zoroastrians turned to the Nestorian Church to avoid Islam, or reconceptualized Zoroaster as a prophet sent to a community with a Book. With the *dhimmī* system (the system of protecting non-Muslims for payment), Muslim rulers formalized and probably intensified pre-Islamic tendencies toward religious communalization. Furthermore, the greater formality of the new system could protect the subject communities from each other as well as from the dominant minority. So "converting" to Islam, at least in the Nile-to-Oxus region, meant joining one recognizably distinct social entity and leaving another. One of the most significant aspects of many Muslim societies was the inseparability of "religious" affiliation and group membership, a phenomenon that has translated poorly into the social structures of modern Muslim nations. In the central caliphal lands of the early 8th century, membership in the Muslim community offered the best chance for social and physical mobility, regardless of a certain degree of discrimination against non-Arabs. Among many astounding examples of this mobility is the fact that several of the early governors and independent dynasts of Egypt and the Maghrib were grandsons of men born in Central Asia.

The Marwānid Maghrib illustrates a kind of conversion more like that of the peninsular Arabs. After the defeat of initial Amazigh resistance movements, the Arab conquerors of the Maghrib quickly incorporated the Amazigh tribes en masse into the Muslim community, turning them immediately to further conquests. In 710 an Arab-Amazigh army set out for the Iberian Peninsula under the leadership of Ṭāriq ibn Ziyād (the name Gibraltar is derived from Jabal Ṭāriq, or "Mountain of Ṭāriq"). They defeated King Roderick in 711; raided into and through the Iberian Peninsula, which they called al-Andalūs; and ruled in the name of the Umayyad caliph. The Andalusian Muslims never had serious goals across the Pyrenees. In 732 Charles Martel encountered not a Muslim army but a summer raiding party; despite his "victory" over that party, Muslims continued their seasonal raiding along the southern French coast for many years.

Muslim Andalusia is particularly interesting because there the pressure for large-scale conversion that was coming to plague the

In Andalusia, Muslim rule did not lead to large-scale conversions, but it did lead to the emergence of Mozarabs, Spanish Christians who adopted Arabic language and culture. This illustration from a copy of the *Cantigas de Santa María* shows Christian slaves herded forward by Muslim foot soldiers.

Umayyads in Syria, Iraq, and Iran never developed. Muslims may never have become a majority throughout their 700-year Andalusian presence. Non-Muslims entered into the Muslim realm as Mozarabs, Christians who had adopted the language and manners, rather than the faith, of the Arabs. Given essentially the same administrative arrangements, the Iberian Christian population was later restored to dominance while the Syrian Christian population was drastically reduced, but the Iberian Jewish population all but disappeared while the Nile-to-Oxus Jewish population survived.

The Imazighen who remained in the Maghrib illustrate the mobility of ideologies and institutions from the central lands to more recently conquered territories. No sooner had they given up anti-Muslim resistance and joined the Muslim community than they rebelled again, but this time an Islamic identity, Kharijism, provided the justification. Kharijite ideas had been carried to the Maghrib by refugees from the numerous revolts against the Marwānids. Kharijite egalitarianism suited the economic and social grievances of the Imazighen as non-Arab Muslims under Arab rule. The revolts outlasted the Marwānids; they resulted in the first independent Maghribi dynasty, the Rustamid, founded by Muslims of Persian descent. The direct influence of the revolts was felt as late as the 10th century and survives among small communities in Tunisia and Algeria.

The Third *Fitnah*

Meanwhile, in the central caliphal lands, growing discontent with the emerging order crystallized in a multifaceted movement of opposition to the Marwānids. It culminated in the third *fitnah* (744–750), which resulted in the establishment of a new and final dynasty of caliphs, the ʿAbbāsids. Ever since the second *fitnah*, a number of concerned and self-conscious Muslims had begun to raise serious questions about the proper Muslim life and the Marwānids' ability to exemplify it, and to answer them by reference to key events in the *ummah*'s history. Pious Muslims tried to define a good Muslim and to decide whether a bad Muslim should be excluded from the community, or a bad caliph from office. They also considered God's role in determining a person's sinfulness and final dispensation. The proper relationship between Arab and non-Arab Muslims, and between Muslims and *dhimmīs*, was another important and predictable focus of reflection. The willingness of non-Arabs to join the *ummah* was growing, but the Marwānids had not found a solution that was either ideologically acceptable or fiscally sound. Because protected non-Muslim groups paid special taxes, fiscal stability seemed to depend on continuing to discourage conversion. One Marwānid, ʿUmar II (ruled 717–720), experimented unsuccessfully with a just solution. In these very practical and often pressing debates lay the germs of Muslim theology, as various overlapping positions, not always coterminous with political groupings, were taken: rejecting the history of the community by demanding rule by Muhammad's family; rejecting the history of the community by following any pious Muslim and excluding any sinner; or accepting the history of the community, its leaders, and most of its members.

In the course of these debates the Marwānid caliphs began to seem severely deficient to a significant number of Muslims of differing persuasions and aspirations. Direct and implied criticism began to surface. Al-Ḥasan al-Baṣrī, a pious ascetic and a model for the early Sufis, called on the Marwānids to rule as good Muslims and called on good Muslims to be suspicious of worldly power. Ibn Isḥāq composed an account of Muhammad's messengership that emphasized the importance of the *anṣār*, the Yathribi tribes that accepted Muhammad, and by implication the non-Arab converts (from whom Ibn Isḥāq himself was descended). The Marwānids were accused of *bidʿah*, new actions for which there were no legitimate Islamic precedents. Their continuation of pre-Islamic institutions—the spy system, extortion of deposed officials by torture, and summary execution—were some of their most visible "offenses." To the pious, the ideal ruler, or imam (the word also for a Muslim who led the *ṣalāt*), should, like Muhammad, possess special learning and knowledge. The first four caliphs, they argued, had been imams in this sense, but under the Umayyads the caliphate had been reduced to a military and administrative office devoid of *imāmah*, of true legitimacy. This piety-minded opposition to the Umayyads, as it has been aptly dubbed, now began to talk about a new dispensation. Some of the most vocal members found special learning and knowledge only in Muhammad's family. Some defined Muhammad's family broadly to include any Hāshimite; others, more narrowly, to include only descendants of ʿAlī. As the number of Muhammad's descendants through ʿAlī had grown, numerous rebellions had broken out in the name of one or the other, drawing on various combinations of constituencies and reflecting a wide spectrum of Islamic and pre-Islamic aspirations.

In the late Marwānid period, the piety-minded opposition found expression in a movement organized in Khorāsān (Khurasan) by Abū Muslim, a semisecret operative of one particularly ambitious Hāshimite family, the ʿAbbāsids. The ʿAbbāsids, who were kin but not descendants of Muhammad, claimed also to have inherited, a generation earlier, the authority of one of ʿAlī's actual descendants, Abū Hāshim. Publicly Abū Muslim called for any qualified member of Muhammad's family to become caliph, but privately he allowed the partisans (*shīʿah*) of ʿAlī to assume that he meant them. Abū Muslim ultimately succeeded because he managed to link the concerns of the piety-minded in Syria and Iraq with Khorāsānian discontent. He played upon the grievances of its Arab tribes against the tribes of Syria and their representatives in the Khorāsānian provincial government, and on the millennial expectations of non-Arab converts and non-Muslims disenchanted with the injustices of Marwānid rule.

When in 750 the army organized and led by Abū Muslim succeeded in defeating the last Marwānid ruler, his caliph-designate represented only one segment of this broad coalition. He was the head of the ʿAbbāsid family, Abū al-ʿAbbās al-Saffāḥ, who now subordinated the claims of the party of ʿAlī to those of his own family and who promised to restore the unity of thc *ummah*, or *jamāʿah*. The circumstances of his accession reconfigured the piety-minded opposition that had helped bring him to power. The party of ʿAlī refused to accept the compromise the ʿAbbāsids offered. Their former fellow opponents did accept membership in the reunified *jamāʿah*, isolating the People of the Shīʿah and causing them to define themselves in terms of more radical points of view. Those who accepted the early ʿAbbāsids came to be known as the People of the Sunnah and Jamāʿah. They accepted the cumulative historical reality of the *ummah's* first century: all the decisions of the community and all the caliphs it had accepted had been legitimate, as would be any subsequent caliph who could unite the community. The concept of *fitnah* acquired a fully historicist meaning: if internal discord were a trial sent by God, then any unifying victor must be God's choice.

SUNNIS AND SHĪʿITES

The historicists came to be known as Sunnis and their main opponents as Shīʿites. These labels are somewhat misleading because they imply that only the Sunnis tried to follow the Sunnah of Muhammad. In fact, each group relied on the Sunnah but emphasized different elements. For the Sunnis, who should more properly be called the Jamāʿī-Sunnis, the principle of solidarity was essential to the Sunnah. The Shīʿites

باد از کار مروان فارغ کرد و چه در حیات او و این کار او دست و او را سقامت گیرد و چون او کرت

ساید و این کار بی مخاصم و منازع بدست آید ابوالعباس عذر او را بقول کرد و او را ابلوی

دجند انک کار او را مستقیم شد ابو سلمه را از پیش برداشت و این قصه در تواریخ بچند نوع آ

Muslims proclaim their allegiance to Abū al-ʿAbbās al-Saffāḥ, the first of the ʿAbbāsid caliphs.

argued that the fundamental element of the Sunnah, and one willfully overlooked by the Jamāʿī-Sunnis, was Muhammad's devotion to his family and his wish that they succeed him through ʿAlī. These new labels expressed and consolidated the social reorganization that had been under way since the beginning of the conquests. The vast majority of Muslims now became consensus-oriented, while a small minority became oppositional. The inherent inimitability of Muhammad's role had made it impossible for any form of successorship to capture universal approval.

When the ʿAbbāsids denied the special claims of the family of ʿAlī, they prompted the Shīʿites to define themselves as a permanent opposition to the status quo. The crystallization of Shīʿism into a movement of protest received its greatest impetus during and just after the lifetime of one of the most influential Shīʿite leaders of the early ʿAbbāsid period, Jaʿfar al-Ṣādiq (died 765). Jaʿfar's vision and leadership allowed the Shīʿites to understand their chaotic history as a meaningful series of efforts by truly pious and suffering Muslims to right the wrongs of the majority. The leaders of the minority had occupied the office of imam, the central Shīʿite institution, which had been passed on from the first imam, ʿAlī, by designation down to Jaʿfar, the sixth. To protect his followers from increasing Sunni hostility to the views of radical Shīʿites, known as the *ghulāt* ("extremists"), who claimed prophethood for ʿAlī, Jaʿfar made a distinction that both protected the uniqueness of prophethood and established the superiority of the role of imam. Since prophethood had ended, its true intent would die without the imams, whose protection from error allowed them to carry out their indispensable task.

Although Jaʿfar did develop an ideology that invited Sunni toleration, he did not unify all Shīʿites. Differences continued to be expressed through loyalty to various of his relatives. During Jaʿfar's lifetime, his uncle Zayd revolted in Kūfah (740), founding the branch of Shīʿism known as the Zaydiyyah (Zaydis), or Fivers (for their allegiance to the fifth imam), who became particularly important in southern Arabia. Any pious follower of ʿAlī could become their imam, and any imam could be deposed if he behaved unacceptably. The Shīʿite majority followed Jaʿfar's son Mūsā al-Kāẓim and imams in his line through the 12th, who disappeared in 873. Those loyal to the 12 imams became known as the Imāmīs or Ithnā ʿAshariyyah (Twelvers). They adopted a quietistic stance toward the status quo government of the ʿAbbāsids and prepared to wait until the 12th imam should return as the messiah to avenge injustices against Shīʿites and to restore justice before the Last Judgment. Some of Jaʿfar's followers, however, remained loyal to Ismāʿīl, Jaʿfar's eldest son who predeceased his father after being designated. These became the Ismāʿīliyyah (Ismāʿīlīs) or Sabʿiyyah (Seveners), and they soon became a source of continuing revolution in the name of Ismāʿīl's son Muḥammad al-Tamm, who was believed to have disappeared. Challenges to the ʿAbbāsids were not long in coming; of particular significance was the establishment in 789 of the first independent Shīʿite dynasty, in present-day Morocco, by Idrīs ibn ʿAbd Allāh ibn Ḥasan II, who had fled after participating in an unsuccessful uprising near Mecca. Furthermore, Kharijite rebellions continued to occur regularly.

The ʿAbbāsids

Legitimacy was a scarce and fragile resource in all premodern societies; in the early ʿAbbāsid environment, competition to define and secure legitimacy was especially intense. The ʿAbbāsids came to power vulnerable; their early actions undermined the unitive potential of their office. Having alienated the Shīʿites, they liquidated the Umayyad family, one of whom, ʿAbd al-Raḥmān I, escaped and founded his own state in Andalusia. Although the ʿAbbāsids were able to buttress their legitimacy by employing the force of their Khorāsānian army, by appealing to their piety-minded support, and by emphasizing their position as heirs to the pre-Islamic traditions of rulership, their own circumstances and policies militated against them. Despite their continuing preference for Khorāsānian troops, the ʿAbbāsids' move to Iraq and their execution of Abū Muslim disappointed the Khorāsānian chauvinists who had helped them. The non-Muslim majority often rebelled too. Bihʾāfrīd ibn Farwardīn claimed to be a prophet capable of incorporating both Zoroastrianism and Islam into a new faith. Hāshim ibn Ḥākim, called al-Muqannaʿ ("the Veiled One"), around 759 declared himself a prophet and then a god, heir to all previous prophets, to numerous followers of ʿAlī, and to Abū Muslim himself.

The ʿAbbāsids symbolized their connection with their pre-Islamic predecessors by founding a new capital, Baghdad, near the old Sāsānian capital. They also continued to elaborate the Sāsānian-like structure begun by the Marwānid governors in Iraq. Their court life became more and more elaborate, the bureaucracy fuller, the inner sanctum of the palace fuller than ever with slaves and concubines as well as the retinues of the caliph's four legal wives. By the time of Hārūn al-Rashīd (ruled 786–809), Europe had nothing to compare with Baghdad, not even the court of his contemporary Charlemagne (ruled 768–814). But problems surfaced too. Slaves' sons fathered by Muslims were not slaves and so could compete for the succession. Despite the ʿAbbāsids' defense of Islam, unconverted Jews and Christians could be influential at court. The head (vizier, or *wazīr*) of the financial bureaucracy sometimes became the effective head of government by taking over the chancery as well. Like all absolute rulers, the ʿAbbāsid caliphs soon confronted the insoluble dilemma of absolutism: the monarch cannot be absolute unless he depends on helpers, but his dependence on helpers undermines his absolutism.

In 762, al-Manṣūr, the second ʿAbbāsid caliph, founded the new capital of Baghdad, which he called Madīnat al-Salām ("City of Peace"). The capital was constructed within circular walls and called "the Round City."

Hārūn al-Rashīd experienced this paradox in a particularly painful way: having drawn into his service prominent members of a family of Buddhist converts, the Barmakids, he found them such rivals that he liquidated them within a matter of years. It was also during Hārūn's reign that Ibrāhīm ibn al-Aghlab, a trusted governor in Tunis, founded a dynasty that gradually became independent, as did the Ṭāhirids, the ʿAbbāsid governors in Khorāsān, two decades later.

The ʿAbbāsids' ability to rival their pre-Islamic predecessors was enhanced by their generous patronage of artists and artisans of all kinds. The great 7,000-mile Silk Road from Ch'ang-an (now Xi'an [Sian], China) to Baghdad—then the two largest cities in the world—helped provide the wealth. The ensuing literary florescence was promoted by the capture of a group of Chinese papermakers at the Battle of Talas in 751. The ʿAbbāsids encouraged translation from pre-Islamic languages, particularly Middle Persian, Greek, and Syriac. This activity provided a channel through which older thought could enter and be reoriented by Islamicate societies. In the field of mathematics, al-Khwārizmī, from whose name the word algorithm is derived, creatively combined Hellenistic and Sanskritic concepts. The word *algebra* derives from the title of his major work, *Kitāb al-jabr wa al-muqābala*h ("The Book of Integration and Equation"). Movements such as *falsafah* (a combination of the positive sciences with logic and metaphysics) and *kalām* (systematic theological discourse) applied Hellenistic thought to new questions. The translation of Indo-Persian lore promoted the development of *adab*, a name for a sophisticated prose literature as well as the set of refined urbane manners that characterized its clientele. Soon a movement called *shu ʿūbiyyah* arose to champion the superiority of non-Arabic tastes over the alleged crudeness of the poetry so dear to Arabic litterateurs. However, the great writer of early ʿAbbāsid times, al-Jāḥiẓ, produced a type of

THE SILK ROAD

The Silk Road is an ancient trade route that, linking China with the West, carried goods and ideas between the two great civilizations of Rome and China. Silk came westward, while wools, gold, and silver went east. China also received Nestorian Christianity and Buddhism (from India) via the road. Originating at Xi'an (Sian), the 4,000-mile (6,400-km) road, actually a caravan tract, followed the Great Wall of China to the northwest, bypassed the Takla Makan Desert, climbed the Pamirs (mountains), crossed Afghanistan, and went on to the Levant; from there the merchandise was shipped across the Mediterranean Sea. Few persons traveled the entire route, and goods were handled in a staggered progression by middlemen.

With the gradual loss of Roman territory in Asia and the rise of Arabian power in the Levant, the Silk Road became increasingly unsafe and untraveled. In the 13th and 14th centuries the route was revived under the Mongols, and at that time the Venetian Marco Polo used the road to travel to Cathay (China). It is now widely thought that the route was one of the main ways that plague bacteria responsible for the Black Death pandemic in Europe in the mid-14th century moved westward from Asia.

The road now partially exists in the form of a paved highway connecting Pakistan and the Uygur Autonomous Region of Xinjiang, China. The old road has been the impetus behind a United Nations plan for a trans-Asian highway, and a railway counterpart of the road has been proposed by the UN Economic and Social Commission for Asia and the Pacific (UNESCAP). The road inspired cellist Yo-Yo Ma to found the Silk Road Project in 1999, which explored cultural traditions along its route and beyond as a means for connecting arts worldwide across cultures.

adab that fused pre-Islamic and Islamic concerns in excellent Arabic style. Many of these extra-Islamic resources conflicted with Islamic expectations. Ibn al-Muqaffaʿ, an administrator under al-Manṣūr (ruled 754–775), urged his master to emulate pre-Islamic models, lest the law that the religious specialists (the ulama) were developing undermine caliphal authority irrevocably.

The ʿAbbāsids never acted on such advice completely; they even contravened it by appealing for piety-minded support. Having encouraged conversion, they tried to "purify" the Muslim community of what they perceived to be socially dangerous and alien ideas. Al-Mahdī (ruled 775–785) actively persecuted the Manichaeans, whom he defined as heretics so as to deny them status as a protected community. He also tried to identify Manichaeans who had joined the Muslim community without abandoning their previous ideas and practices. ʿAbbāsid "purification of Islam" ironically coincided with some of the most significant absorption of pre-Islamic monotheistic lore to date, as illustrated by the stories of the prophets written by Al-Kisāʾī, grammarian and tutor to a royal prince. Even though, like the Marwānids, the ʿAbbāsids continued to maintain administrative courts, not accessible to the *qāḍīs*, they also promoted the study of *ʿilm* and the status of those who pursued it. In so doing they fostered what Ibn al-Muqaffaʿ had feared—the emergence of an independent body of law, Sharīʿah, which Muslims could use to evaluate and circumvent caliphal rule itself.

SHARĪʿAH

A key figure in the development of Sharīʿah was Abū ʿAbd Allāh al-Shāfiʿī, who died in 820. By his time Islamic law was extensive but uncoordinated, reflecting differing local needs and tastes. Schools had begun to form around various recognized masters, such as al-Awzaʿī in Syria, Abū Ḥanīfah in Iraq, and Mālik ibn Anas, all of whom used some combination of local custom, personal reasoning, Qurʾān, and Hadith. Al-Shāfiʿī was raised in Mecca, studied with Mālik, participated in a Shīʿite revolt in the Yemen, and was sent to Baghdad as a prisoner of the caliph. After his release he emigrated to Egypt, where he produced his most famous work. Like most other *faqīhs* (students of jurisprudence, or *fiqh*), al-Shāfiʿī viewed Muhammad's community as a social ideal and his first four successors as rightly guided. So that this exemplary time could provide the basis for Islamic law, he constructed a hierarchy of legal sources: Qurʾān; Hadith, clearly traceable to Muhammad and in some cases to his companions; *ijmāʿ* (consensus); and *qiyās* (analogy to one of the first three).

The way in which Islamic law had developed had allowed many pre-Islamic customs, such as the veiling and seclusion of women, to receive a sanction not given to them in the Qurʾān or the Hadith.

For his efforts in codifying Islamic law, or Sharīʿah, al-Shāfiʿī is often called the father of Muslim jurisprudence. Shown is the mosque in Cairo, Egypt, that contains al-Shāfiʿī's mausoleum.

Al-Shāfiʿī did not change that entirely. Law continued to be pursued in different centres, and several major "ways" (*madhhabs*) began to coalesce among Sunnis and Shīʿites alike. Among Sunnis, four schools came to be preeminent—Shāfiʿiyyah (Shafiites), Mālikiyyah (Malikites), Ḥanafiyyah (Hanafites), and Ḥanābilah (Hanbalites)—and each individual Muslim was expected to restrict himself to only one. Furthermore, the notion that the gate of *ijtihād* (personal effort at reasoning) closed in the 9th century was not firmly established until the 12th century. However, al-Shāfiʿī's system was widely influential in controlling divergence and in limiting undisciplined forms of personal reasoning. It also stimulated the collecting and testing of hadiths for their unbroken traceability to Muhammad or a companion. The need to verify Hadith stimulated a characteristic form of premodern Muslim intellectual and literary activity, the collecting of biographical materials into compendiums (*ṭabaqāt*). By viewing the Qurʾān and documentable Sunnah as preeminent, al-Shāfiʿī also undermined those in ʿAbbāsid court circles who wanted a more flexible base from which the caliph could operate. The Sharīʿah came to be a supremely authoritative, comprehensive set of norms and rules covering every aspect of life, from worship to personal hygiene. It applied equally to all Muslims, including the ruler, whom Sharīʿah-minded Muslims came to view as its protector, not its administrator or developer. While the caliphs were toying with theocratic notions of themselves as the shadow of God on earth, the students of legal knowledge were defining their rule as "nomocratic," based only on the law they protected and enforced.

According to the Sharīʿah, a Muslim order was one in which the ruler was Muslim and the Sharīʿah was enshrined as a potential guide to all; Muslims were one confessional community among many, each of which would have its own laws that would apply except in disputes between members of different communities. The Sharīʿah regulated relations and inequities among different segments of society—freeborn Muslim, slave, and protected non-Muslim. The process that produced Sharīʿah resembled the evolution of oral Torah and rabbinic law, which the Sharīʿah resembled in its comprehensiveness, egalitarianism, and consensualism, in its absorption of local custom, in its resistance to distinguishing the sublime from the mundane, and in its independence from government. Like many Jews, many ultra-pious Muslims came to view the law as a divine rather than human creation.

THE FOURTH *FITNAH*

During the reign of al-Maʾmūn (813–833) the implications of all this *ʿilm*-based activity for caliphal authority began to become clear. Al-Maʾmūn came to the caliphate as the result of the fourth *fitnah*, which reflected the persisting alienation of Khorāsān. Al-Maʾmūn's father, Hārūn al-Rashīd, provided for the empire to be divided at his death between two sons. Al-Amīn would rule in the capital and all the western domains, and al-Maʾmūn, from his provincial seat at Merv in Khorāsān, would rule the less significant east. When Hārūn died, his sons struggled to expand their control. Al-Maʾmūn won. During his reign, which probably represents the high point of caliphal absolutism, the court intervened in an unprecedented manner in the intellectual life of its Muslim subjects, who for the next generation engaged in the first major intra-Muslim conflict that focused on belief

This 16th-century Indian illustration depicts subjects paying allegiance to al-Maʿmūn, who rose to the caliphate as a result of the fourth *fitnah*.

as well as practice. The Muslims, who now constituted a much more sizable proportion of the population but whose faith lacked doctrinal clarity, began to engage in an argument reminiscent of 2nd-century Christian discussions of the Logos. Among Christians, for whom the Word was Jesus, the argument had taken a Christological form. But for Muslims the argument had to centre on the Qurʾān and its created or uncreated nature. Al-Maʾmūn, as well as his brother and successor al-Muʿtaṣim (833–842), was attracted to the Muʿtazilah (Mutazilites), whose school had been influenced by Hellenistic ideas as well as by contact with non-Muslim theologians. If the Qurʾān were eternal along with God, his unity would, for the Muʿtazilah, be violated. They especially sought to avoid literal exegesis of the Qurʾān, which in their view discouraged free will and produced embarrassing inconsistencies and anthropomorphisms. By arguing that the Qurʾān was created in time, they could justify metaphorical and changing interpretation. By implication, Muhammad's position as deliverer of revelation was undermined because Hadith was made less authoritative.

The opponents of the Muʿtazilah, and therefore of the official position, coalesced around the figure of Aḥmad ibn Ḥanbal. A leading master of Hadith, he had many followers, some of them recent converts, whom he was able to mobilize in large public demonstrations against the doctrine of the created Qurʾān. Because viewing the Qurʾān as created would invalidate its absolute authority, Ibn Ḥanbal argued for an eternal Qurʾān and emphasized the importance of Muhammad's Sunnah to the understanding of it. By his time, major literary works had established a coherent image of the indispensability of Muhammad's prophethood; in fact, just before the Muʿtazilite controversy began, Ibn Hishām had produced his classic recension of the *sīrah*, or life, of Muhammad, composed half a century earlier by Ibn Isḥāq. As in the early Christian church, these were not merely dogmatic issues. They were rooted in the way ordinary Muslims lived, just as affection for a divine Christ had become popular sentiment by the time Arius and Athanasius debated. Although Muslims lacked an equivalent of the Christian church, they resolved these issues similarly. Like Jesus for the Christians, the Qurʾān for the Muslims was somehow part of God. Hadith-mindedness and emulation of Muhammad's Sunnah had become such an essential part of the daily life of ordinary people that the Muʿtazilite position, as intellectually consistent and attractive as it was, was unmarketable. In a series of forcible inquiries called *miḥnah*, al-Maʾmūn and al-Muʿtaṣim actively persecuted those who, like Ibn Ḥanbal, would not conform, but popular sentiment triumphed, and after al-Muʿtaṣim's death the caliph al-Mutawakkil was forced to reverse the stand of his predecessors.

This caliphal failure to achieve doctrinal unity coincided with other crises. By al-Muʿtaṣim's reign the tribal troops were becoming unreliable and the Ṭāhirid governors of Khorāsān more independent. Al-Muʿtaṣim expanded his use of military slaves, finding them more loyal but more unruly too. Soon he had to house them at Sāmarrāʾ, a new capital north of Baghdad, where the caliphate remained until 892. For most of this period, the caliphs were actually under the control of their slave soldiery, and, even though they periodically reasserted their authority, rebellions continued. Many were anti-Muslim, like that of the Iranian Bābak (whose 20-year-long revolt was crushed in 837), but increasingly they were intra-Muslim, like the Kharijite-led revolt of black agricultural slaves (Zanj) in southern Iraq (869–883). By 870 then, the Baghdad-Sāmarrāʾ caliphate had become one polity among many; its real rulers had no ideological legitimacy. At Córdoba the Umayyads had declared their independence, and the Maghrib was divided among several dynasties of differing persuasions—the Shīʿite Idrīsids, the Kharijite Rustamids, and the Jamāʿī-Sunni Aghlabids. The former governors of the ʿAbbāsids, the Ṭūlūnids, ruled Egypt and parts of Arabia. Iran was divided between the Ṣaffārids, governors of the ʿAbbāsids in the south, and the Persian Sāmānids in the north.

The centrifugal forces represented by these administrative divisions should not obscure, however, the existence of numerous centripetal forces that continued to give Islamdom, from Andalusia to Central Asia, other types of unity. The ideal of the caliphate continued to be a source of unity after the reality waned; among all the new states, no alternative to the caliphate could replace it. Furthermore, now that Muslims constituted a majority almost everywhere in Islamdom, conflict began to be expressed almost exclusively in Islamic rather than anti-Islamic forms. In spite of continuing intra-Muslim conflict, Muslim worship and belief remained remarkably uniform. The annual pilgrimage to Mecca helped reinforce this underlying unity by bringing disparate Muslims together in a common rite. The pilgrimage, as well as the rise of prosperous regional urban centres, enhanced the trade that traversed Islamdom regardless of political conflicts; along the trade routes that crisscrossed Eurasia, Islamdom at its centre, moved not only techniques and goods but ideas as well. A network of credit and banking, caravansaries, and intercity mercantile alliances tied far-flung regions together. Central was the caravan, then the world's most effective form of transport. The peripatetic nature of education promoted cross-fertilization. Already the *faqīr* (fakir), a wandering Sufi dervish who lives by begging, was a familiar traveler. Across Islamdom, similar mosque-market complexes sprang up in most towns; because municipal institutions were rare, political stability so unpredictable, and government intervention kept to a minimum (sometimes by design, more often by necessity), the Sharīʿah and the learned men who carried it became a mainstay of everyday life and social intercourse. The Sharīʿah, along with the widespread affection for the Sunnah of Muhammad, regulated, at least among pious Muslims, personal habits of the most specific sort, from the use of scent to the cut of a beard. Comprehensive and practical, the Sunnah could amuse as well. When asked whether to trust in God or tie one's camel, so a popular hadith goes, the Prophet replied, "Trust in God, then tie your camel."

The significance of Hadith and Sunnah is represented by the ending date of the period of conversion and crystallization. No one can say exactly when the majority of Islamdom's population became Muslim. Older scholarship looks to the end of the first quarter of the 9th century, newer scholarship to the beginning of the third quarter. In 870 a man died whose life's work symbolized the consolidation of Islam in everyday life: al-Bukhārī, who produced one of the six collections of Hadith recognized as authoritative by Jamāʿī-Sunni Muslims. His fellow collector of Hadith, Muslim ibn al-Ḥajjāj, died about four years later. About the same time, classical thinkers in other areas of Islamicate civilization died, among them the great author of *adab*, al-Jāḥiẓ (died 868/869), the great early ecstatic Sufis Abū al-Fayḍ Dhū al-Nūn al-Miṣrī (died 861) and Abū Yazīd Bisṭāmī (died 874), the philosopher Yaʿqūb ibn Isḥaq al-Ṣabāḥ al-Kindī (died c. 870), and the historian of the conquests al-Balādhurī (died c. 892). Men of different religious and ethnic heritages, they signified by the last quarter of the 9th century the full and varied range of intellectual activities of a civilization that had come of age.

CHAPTER 4

FRAGMENTATION AND FLORESCENCE (870–1041)

The unifying forces operative at the end of the period of conversion and crystallization persisted during the period of fragmentation and florescence, but the caliphal lands in Iraq became less central. Even though Baghdad remained preeminent in cultural prestige, important initiatives were being taken from surrounding regions: Andalusia; the Maghrib and sub-Saharan Africa; Egypt, Syria, and the holy cities (Mecca and Medina); Iraq; and Iran, Afghanistan, Transoxania (an historical region roughly corresponding to present-day Uzbekistan and parts of Turkmenistan, Tajikistan, and Kazakhstan), and, toward the end of the period, northern India. Regional courts could compete with the ʿAbbāsids and with each other as patrons of culture. Interregional and intra-regional conflicts were often couched in terms of loyalties formed in the period of conversion and crystallization, but local history provided supplemental identities. Although the ʿAbbāsid caliphate was still a focus of concern and debate, other forms of leadership became important. Just as being Muslim no longer meant being Arab, being cultured no longer meant speaking and writing exclusively in Arabic. Certain Muslims began to cultivate a second language of high culture, New Persian. As in pre-Islamic times, written as well as spoken bilingualism became important. Ethnic differences were blurred by the effects of peripatetic education and shared languages. Physical mobility was so common that many individuals lived and

With the rise of New Persian as a language of high culture emerged important literature such as the poetry of Jalāl al-Dīn Rūmī.

died far from their places of birth. Cultural creativity was so noticeable that this period is often called the Renaissance of Islam.

Economic changes also promoted regional strengths. Although Baghdad continued to profit from its central location, caliphal neglect of Iraq's irrigation system and southerly shifts in the trans-Asian trade promoted the fortunes of Egypt; the opening of the Sahara to Maghribi Muslims provided a new source of slaves, salt, and minerals; and Egyptian expansion into the Mediterranean opened a major channel for Islamicate influence on medieval Europe. Islamdom continued to expand, sometimes as the result of aggression on the part of frontier warriors (*ghāzīs*) but more often as the result of trade. The best symbol of this expansiveness is Ibn Faḍlān, who left a provocative account of his mission in 921, on behalf of the Baghdad caliph, to the Volga Bulgars, among whom he met Swedes coming down the river to trade.

By the beginning of the period of fragmentation and florescence, the subject populations of most Muslim rulers were predominantly Muslim, and nonsedentary peoples had ceased to play a major role. The period gave way to a much longer period (dated 1041–1405) in which migratory tribal peoples were once again critically important. In 1041 the reign of the Ghaznavid sultan Masʿūd I ended; by then the Ghaznavid state had lost control over the Seljuq Turks in their eastern Iranian domains and thus inaugurated Islamdom's second era of tribal expansion. Because localism and cosmopolitanism coexisted in the period of fragmentation and florescence, the period is best approached through a region-by-region survey that underscores phenomena of interregional significance.

Andalusia, the Maghrib, and Sub-Saharan Africa

Andalusia, far from the centre of Islamdom, illustrated the extent of ʿAbbāsid prestige and the assertion of local creativity. In the beginning of the period, Islamicate rule was represented by the Umayyads at Córdoba; established in 756 by ʿAbd al-Raḥmān I (known as al-Dākhil, "the Immigrant"), a refugee from the ʿAbbāsid victory over the Syrian Umayyads, the Umayyad dynasty in Córdoba replaced a string of virtually independent deputies of the Umayyad governors in the Maghrib. At first the Cordoban Umayyads had styled themselves emirs, the title also used by caliphal governors and other local rulers; though refugees from ʿAbbāsid hostility, they continued to mention the ʿAbbāsids in the Friday worship session until 773. Their independence was not made official, however, until their best-known member, ʿAbd al-Raḥmān III (ruled 912–961), adopted the

ʿAbd al-Raḥmān III.

title of caliph in 929 and began having the Friday prayer recited in the name of his own house.

The fact that ʿAbd al-Raḥmān declared his independence from the ʿAbbāsids while he modeled his court after theirs illustrates the period's cultural complexities. Like that of the ʿAbbāsids and the Marwānids, ʿAbd al-Raḥmān's absolute authority was limited by the nature of his army (Amazigh tribesmen and Slav slaves) and by

EMIR

An emir (in Arabic: *Amīr*, "commander," or "prince") is an Islamic title used for a military commander, governor of a province, or a high military official. Under the Umayyads, the emir exercised administrative and financial powers, somewhat diminished under the ʿAbbāsids, who introduced a separate financial officer. Sometimes, as in the cases of the Aghlabids and Ṭāhirids, the emirs ruled virtually independently in their provinces with but token allegiance to the caliph. In other cases the province was first taken by force, then the emirs applied for legitimacy to the caliph.

The title *amīr al-muʾminīn*, sometimes used of leaders of Muslim military campaigns, was assumed by ʿUmar, the second caliph, probably on the basis of the Qurʾānic "Obey God and obey the Apostle and those invested with command (*ūlī al-amr*) among you" (iv, 59); it was used by all his successors until the abolition of the caliphate in 1924.

In the 10th century the commander of the caliph's armies at Baghdad was styled *amīr al-umarāʾ* ("commander in chief"). Emir could also denote office, as in *amīr al-ḥājj*, "leader of the pilgrimage" to Mecca, held by the caliph or his delegate, a precedent set by Abū Bakr and Muḥammad himself (630 and 631).

The title emir was later adopted by the rulers of several independent states in central Asia, notably those of Bukhara and Afghanistan. In the modern United Arab Emirates, however, none of the rulers of the constituent states are called emirs; all are sheikhs. The word Emirates was included in the name of the federation by default, because *mashyakhah* (sheikhdom) was already in use for the smallest of Arab administrative units, comparable to a parish or township.

his dependence on numerous assistants. His internal problems were compounded by external threats, from the Christian kingdoms in the north and the Fāṭimids in the Maghrib. The Umayyad state continued to be the major Muslim presence in the peninsula until 1010, after which time it became, until 1031, but one of many independent city-states. Nowhere is the connection between fragmentation and florescence more evident than in the courts of these *mulūk al-ṭawāʾif*, or "party kings"; it was they who patronized some of Andalusia's most brilliant Islamicate culture. This florescence also demonstrated the permeability of the Muslim-Christian frontier. For example, the poet and theologian Ibn Ḥazm (994–1064) composed love poetry, such as *Ṭawq al-ḥamāmah* (*The Ring of the Dove*), which may have contributed to ideas of chivalric love among the Provençal troubadours.

In 870 the Maghrib was divided among several dynasties, all but one of foreign origin and only one of which, the Aghlabids, nominally represented the ʿAbbāsids. The Muslim Arabs had been very different rulers than any of their predecessors—Phoenicians, Romans, Vandals, or Byzantines—who had occupied but not settled. Their interests in North Africa had been secondary to their objectives in the Mediterranean, so they had restricted themselves to coastal settlements, which they used as staging points for trade with the western Mediterranean or as sources of food for their "metropolitan" population. They had separated themselves from the Imazighen with a fortified frontier. The Arabs, however, forced away from the coast in order to compete more effectively with the Byzantines, had quickly tried to incorporate the Imazighen, who were also pastoralists. One branch of the Imazighen, the Ṣanhājah, extended far into the Sahara, across which they had established a caravan trade with blacks in the Sudanic belt. At some time in the 10th century the Ṣanhājah nominally converted to Islam, and their towns in the Sahara began to assume Muslim characteristics. Around 990 a black kingdom in the Sudan, Ghana, extended itself as far as Audaghost, the Ṣanhājah centre in the Sahara. Thus was black Africa first brought into contact with the Muslim Mediterranean, and thus were the conditions set for dramatic developments in the Maghrib during the 12th and 13th centuries.

In the late 9th century the Maghrib was unified and freed from outside control for the first time. Paradoxically, this independence was achieved by outsiders associated with an international movement of political activism and subversion. Driven underground by ʿAbbāsid intolerance and a maturing ideology of covert revolutionism, the Ismāʿīlī Shīʿites had developed mechanisms to maintain solidarity and undertake political action. These mechanisms can be subsumed under the term *daʿwah*, the same word that had been used for the movement that brought the ʿAbbāsids to power. The *daʿwah's* ability to communicate rapidly over a large area rested on its traveling operatives as well as on a network of local cells. In the late 9th century an Ismāʿīlī movement, nicknamed the Qarāmiṭah (Qarmatians), had seriously but unsuccessfully threatened the ʿAbbāsids in Syria, Iraq, and Bahrain. Seeking other outlets, a Yemeni operative known as Abū ʿAbd Allāh al-Shīʿī made contact, on the occasion of the hajj, with representatives of an Amazigh tribe that had a history of Kharijite hostility to caliphal control. The hajj had already become a major vehicle for tying Islamdom's regions together, and Abū ʿAbd Allāh's movement was only one of many in the Maghrib that would be inaugurated thereby.

In 901 Abū ʿAbd Allāh arrived in Little Kabylia (in present-day Algeria); for eight years he prepared for an imam, preaching of a millennial restoration of justice after an era of foreign oppression. After conquering the Aghlabid capital al-Qayrawān (in present-day Tunisia), he helped free from a Sijilmassa prison his imam, ʿUbayd Allāh, who declared himself the *mahdī*, using a multivalent word that could have quite different meanings for different constituencies. Some Muslims applied *mahdī* to any justice-restoring divinely guided figure; others, including many Jamāʿī-Sunnis, to the apocalyptic figure expected to usher in the millennium before the Last Judgment; and still others, including most Shīʿites, to a returned or restored imam. Abū ʿAbd Allāh's followers may have differed in their expectations, but the *mahdī* himself was unequivocal: he was a descendant of ʿAlī and Fāṭimah through Ismāʿīl's disappeared son and therefore was a continuation of the line of the true imam. He symbolized his victory by founding a new capital named, after himself, al-Mahdiyyah (in present-day Tunisia). During the next half century the "Fāṭimids" tried with limited success to expand westward into the Maghrib and north into the Mediterranean, where they made Sicily a naval base (912–913); but their major goal was Egypt, nominally under ʿAbbāsid control. From Egypt they would challenge the ʿAbbāsid caliphate itself. In 969 the Fāṭimid army conquered the Nile valley and advanced into Palestine and southern Syria as well.

Egypt, Syria, and the Holy Cities

The Fāṭimids established a new and glorious city, Al-Qāhirah ("The Victorious"; Cairo), to rival ʿAbbāsid Baghdad. They then adopted the title of caliph, laying claim to be the legitimate rulers of all Muslims as well as head of all Ismāʿīlīs. Now three caliphs reigned in Islamdom, where there was supposed to be only one. In Cairo the Fāṭimids founded a great mosque-school complex, Al-Azhar. They fostered local handicraft production and revitalized the Red Sea route from India to the Mediterranean. They built up a navy to trade as well as to challenge the Byzantines and underscore the ʿAbbāsid caliph's failure to defend and extend the frontiers. Fāṭimid occupation of the holy cities of Mecca and Medina, complete by the end of the 10th century, had economic as well as spiritual significance: it reinforced the caliph's claim to leadership of all Muslims, provided wealth, and helped him keep watch on the west Arabian coast, from the Hejaz to the Yemen, where a sympathetic Zaydī Shīʿite dynasty had ruled since 897. Fāṭimid presence in the Indian Ocean was even strong enough to establish an Ismāʿīlī missionary in Sind. The Fāṭimids patronized the arts; Fāṭimid glass and ceramics were some of Islamdom's most brilliant. As in other regions, imported styles and tastes were transformed by or supplemented with local artistic impulses, especially in architecture, the most characteristic form of Islamicate art.

The reign of one of the most unusual Fāṭimid caliphs, al-Ḥākim, from 996 to 1021, again demonstrated the interregional character of the Ismāʿīlī movement. Historians describe al-Ḥākim's personal habits as eccentric, mercurial, and unpredictable to the point of cruelty and his religious values as inconsistent with official Ismāʿīlī teachings, tending toward some kind of accommodation with the Jamāʿī-Sunni majority. After he vanished under mysterious circumstances, his religious revisionism was not pursued by his successors or by the Ismāʿīlī establishment in Egypt, but in Syria it inspired a peasant revolt that produced the Druze, who still await al-Ḥākim's return.

When the Fāṭimids expanded into southern Syria, another Shīʿite dynasty, the Ḥamdānids, of Bedouin origin, had been ruling

The city of Cairo was established by the Fāṭimids to rival the ʿAbbāsid capital Baghdad.

northern Syria from Mosul since 905. In 944 a branch of the family had taken Aleppo; under the leadership of their most famous member, Sayf al-Dawlah (ruled c. 943–967), the Ḥamdānids responded aggressively to renewed Byzantine expansionism in eastern Anatolia. They ruled from Aleppo until they were absorbed by the Fāṭimids after 1004; at their court some of Islamdom's most lastingly illustrious writers found patronage. Two notable examples are the poet al-Mutanabbī

(915–965), who illustrated the importance of the poet as a premodern press agent of the court, and al-Fārābī, who tried to reconcile reason and revelation.

Al-Fārābī contributed to the ongoing Islamization of Hellenistic thought. *Falsafah*, the Arabic cognate for the Greek *philosophia*, included metaphysics and logic, as well as the positive sciences, such as mathematics, music, astronomy, and anatomy. *Faylasūf*s often earned their living as physicians, astrologers, or musicians. The *faylasūf*'s whole way of life, like that of the *adīb*, reflected his studies. It was often competitive with that of more self-consciously observant Muslims because the *faylasūf* often questioned the relationship of revelation to real truth. The *faylasūf*s felt free to explore inner truths not exposed to the view of ordinary people; they practiced prudent concealment (*taqiyyah*) of their deeper awareness wherever making it public might endanger the social order. The *faylasūf*s shared the principle of concealment with the Shīʿites; both believed, for rather different reasons, that inner truth was accessible to only a very few. This esotericism had counterparts in all premodern societies, where learning and literacy were severely restricted.

IRAQ

By the late 9th and early 10th centuries the last remnant of the caliphal state was Iraq, under control of the Turkic soldiery. Political decline and instability did not preclude cultural creativity and productivity, however. In fact, Iraq's "generation of 870," loosely construed, contained some of the most striking and lastingly important figures in all of early Islamicate civilization. Three of them illustrate well the range of culture in late 9th- and early 10th-century Iraq: the historian and Qurʾānic exegete al-Ṭabarī (c. 839–923), the theologian Abū al-Ḥasan al-Ashʿarī (c. 873–c. 935), and the ecstatic mystic al-Ḥallāj (c. 858–922).

KEY FIGURES IN IRAQ'S CULTURAL FLOWERING

Al-Ṭabarī was born in Ṭabaristān, south of the Caspian Sea, and as a young man he traveled to Baghdad. Rarely could a man earn his living from religious learning; unless he found patronage, he would probably engage in trade or a craft. All the more astounding was the productivity of scholars like al-Ṭabarī, who said that he produced 40 leaves a day for 40 years. The size of his extant works, which include a commentary on the Qur᾽ān and a universal history, testifies to the accuracy of his claim. His history is unique in sheer size and detail and especially in its long-term impact. His method involved the careful selection, organization, and juxtaposition of separate and often contradictory accounts cast in the form of hadith. This technique celebrated the *ummah's* collective memory and established a range of acceptable disagreement.

Al-Ashʿarī, from Basra, made his contribution to systematic theological discourse (*kalām*). He had been attracted early to a leading Muʿtazilite teacher, but broke away at the age of 40. He went on to use Muʿtazilite methods of reasoning to defend popular ideas such as the eternality and literal truth of the Qur᾽ān and the centrality of Muhammad's Sunnah as conveyed by the Hadith. Where his approach yielded objectionable results, such as an anthropomorphic rendering of God or a potentially polytheistic understanding of his attributes, al-Ashʿarī resorted to the principle of *bilā kayf* ("without regard to the how"), whereby a person of faith accepts that certain fundamentals are true without regard to how they are true and that divine intention is not always accessible to human intelligence. Al-Ashʿarī's harmonization also produced a simple creed, which expressed faith in God, his angels, and his books, and affirmed belief in Muhammad as God's last messenger and in the reality of death, physical resurrection, the Last Judgment, and heaven and hell. Taken together, al-Ṭabarī's historiography and al-Ashʿarī's theology symbolize the consolidation of Jamāʿī-Sunni, Sharīʿah-minded thought and piety.

The most visible and powerful 10th-century exponent of Sufism was al-Ḥallāj. By his day, Sufism had grown far beyond its early forms, which were represented by al-Ḥasan al-Baṣrī (died 728), who practiced *zuhd*, or rejection of the world, and by Rābiʿah al-ʿAdawiyyah (died 801), who formulated the Sufi ideal of a disinterested love of God. The mystics Abū Yazīd Biṣṭāmī (died 874) and Abū al-Qāsim al-Junayd (died 910) had begun to pursue the experience of unity with God, first by being "drunk" with his love and with love of him and then by acquiring life-transforming self-possession and control. Masters (called sheikhs or pīrs) were beginning to attract disciples (*murīds*) to their way. Like other Muslims who tried to go "beyond" the Sharīʿah to inner truth, the Sufis practiced concealment of inner awareness (*taqiyyah*). Al-Ḥallāj, one of al-Junayd's disciples, began to travel and preach publicly, however. His success was disturbing enough for the authorities in Baghdad to have him arrested and condemned to death; he was tortured and beheaded, and finally his body was burned. Yet his career had shown the power of Sufism, which would by the 12th century become an institutionalized form of Islamic piety.

THE BŪYID DYNASTY

Long before, however, a major political change occurred at Baghdad. In 945 control over the caliphs passed from their Turkish soldiery to a dynasty known as the Būyids or Buwayhids. The Būyids came from Daylam, near the southern coast of the Caspian Sea. Living beyond the reach of the caliphs in Baghdad, its residents had identified with Imāmī Shīʿism. By about 930 three sons of a fisherman named Būyeh had emerged as leaders in Daylam. One of them conquered Baghdad, not replacing the caliph but ruling in his name. The fact that they were Shīʿite, as were the Idrīsids, Fāṭimids, and Ḥamdānids, led scholars

Because of his success as a preacher, the Sufi master al-Ḥallāj was eventually crucified and brutally tortured to death. Following his death, his writings and teachings continued to be revered by his devoted followers.

to refer to the period from the mid-10th to mid-11th century as the Shīʿite century.

Like other contemporary rulers, the Būyids were patrons of culture, especially of speculative thought (Shīʿism, Muʿtazilism, *kalām*, and *falsafah*). Jamāʿī-Sunni learning continued to be patronized by the caliphs and their families. The Būyids favoured no one party over another. However, their openness paradoxically invited a hardening in Jamāʿī-Sunni thought. Būyid attempts to maintain the cultural brilliance of the court at Baghdad were limited by a decline in revenue occasioned partly by a shift in trade routes to Fāṭimid Egypt, and partly by long-term neglect of Iraq's irrigation works. The caliphs had occasionally made land assignments (*iqṭā*ʿs) to soldiers in lieu of paying salaries; now the Būyids extended the practice to other individuals and thus removed an important source of revenue from central control. After 983, Būyid territories were split among various members of the family, and pressure was applied to their borders from both the west (by Ḥamdānids and Fāṭimids) and the east (by Sāmānids, Ghaznavids, and Seljuqs).

The economic difficulties of Būyid Iraq promoted urban unrest, accounts of which provide a rare glimpse into the lives of ordinary Muslim town dwellers. Numerous movements served as outlets for socioeconomic grievances, directed most often toward the wealthy or the military. The concentration of wealth in the cities had produced a bipolar stratification system conveyed in the sources by a pair of words, *khāṣṣ* (special) and *ʿāmm* (ordinary). In the environment of 10th- and 11th-century Iraq, an instance of rising food prices or official maltreatment could easily spark riots of varying size, duration, and intensity. Strategies for protest included raiding, looting, and assault. Some movements were more coherently ideological than others, and various forms of piety could reflect socioeconomic distinctions. Some movements were

Beginning in the 970s, infighting became the norm among various members of the Būyid dynasty. Illustrated are ʿAḍud al-Dawlah, the greatest of the Būyid rulers, and Muʾayyad al-Dawlah at war with their brother Fakhr al-Dawlah in the 14th-century manuscript *Jāmiʿ al-tawārīkh* ("Collector of Chronicles") by the Persian historian Rashīd al-Dīn.

particularly attractive to artisans, servants, and soldiers, as was the case with the proponents of Hadith, whose mentor, Aḥmad ibn Ḥanbal (died 855), was viewed as a martyr because of his suffering at the hands of the caliph. Other forms of piety, such as Shīʿism, could be associated with wealthier elements among the landowning and merchant classes.

Beneath the more organized forms of social action lay a more fluid kind of association, most often described by the labels *ʿayyār* and *futuwwah*. These terms refer to individuals acting in concert, as needed, on the basis of certain rough-hewn concepts of proper male public behaviour. Such associations had counterparts in the late Hellenistic world, just as they have parallels in the voluntary protective associations formed in the 19th and 20th centuries whenever official institutions of protection were either chronically or temporarily deficient. For some of the Islamicate "gangs" or "clubs," thuggery may have been the norm; for others, the figure of the fourth caliph and first imam, ʿAlī, seems to have provided an exemplar. Even though Shīʿites had become a separate group with a distinctive interpretation of ʿAlī's significance, a more generalized affection for the family of the Prophet and especially for ʿAlī was widespread among Jamāʿī-Sunnis. ʿAlī had come to be recognized as the archetypal young male (*fatā*); a related word, *futuwwah*, signified groups of young men who pursued such virtues as courage, aiding the weak, generosity, endurance of suffering, love of truth, and hospitality.

Premodern Islamicate societies were characterized by a high degree of fluidity, occasionalism, and voluntarism in the structuring of associations, organizations, loyalties, and occupations. Although all societies must develop ways to maintain social boundaries, ease interaction among groups, and buffer friction, the ways in which Muslim societies have fulfilled these needs seem unusually difficult to delineate. For example, in Muslim cities of the period under discussion, the only official officeholders were appointees of the central government, such as the governor; the *muḥtasib*, a transformed Byzantine *agoranomos* who was monitor of public morality as well as of fair-market practice; or the *ṣāḥib al-shurṭah*, head of the police. In the absence of an organized church or ordained clergy, those whose influence derived from piety or learning were influential because they were recognized as such, not because they were appointed, and men of very different degrees of learning might earn the designation of *ʿālim*. Although the ruler was expected to contribute to the maintenance of public services, neither he nor anyone else was obligated to do so. Though the ruler might maintain prisons for those whose behaviour he disapproved, the local *qāḍīs* had need of none, relying generally on persuasion or negotiation and borrowing the caliphal police on the relatively rare occasion on which someone needed to be brought before them by force. There was no formalized mode of succession for any of the dynasties of the time. Competition, sometimes armed, was relied upon to produce the most qualified candidate.

Patronage was an important basis of social organization. The family served as a premodern welfare agency; where it was absent, minimal public institutions, such as hospitals, provided. One of the most important funding mechanisms for public services was a private one, the *waqf*. The *waqf* provided a legal way to circumvent the Sharīʿah's requirement that an individual's estate be divided among many heirs. Through a waqf, an individual could endow an institution or group with all or part of his estate, in perpetuity, before his death. A *waqf* might provide books for a school, candles or mats for a mosque, salaries of religious functionaries, or land for a hospital or caravansary. *Waqf* money or lands were indivisible, although they might contribute to the welfare of a potential heir who happened to be involved in the *waqf*-supported activity. The *waqf*, like other forms of patronage, provided needed social services without official intervention. On other occasions, wealthy individuals, especially those connected with the ruling family, might simply patronize favourite activities. In addition to patronage, many other overlapping ties bound individual Muslims together: loyalties to an occupation—soldier, merchant, learned man, artisan, government worker—and loyalties to a town or neighbourhood, or to a form of piety, or to persons to whom one made an oath for a specific purpose; and ties to patron or to family, especially foster-parentage (*iṣṭināʿ*), the counterpart of which was significant in medieval Christendom.

The Qurʾān and Sharīʿah discouraged corporate responsibility in favour of individual action; even the legal scope of partnership was limited. Yet the unstable political realities that had militated against the emergence of broad-based institutions sometimes called for corporate action, as when a city came to terms with a new ruler or invader. In those cases, a vaguely defined group of notables, known usually as *aʿyān*, might come together to represent their city in negotiations, only to cease corporate action when the more functional small-group loyalties could safely be resumed. Within this shifting frame of individuals and groups, the ruler was expected to maintain a workable, if not equitable, balance. More often than not the real ruler was a local *amīr* of some sort. For this reason, the de facto system of rule that emerged during this period, despite the persistence of the central caliphate in Baghdad, has sometimes been referred to as the aʿ*yān-amīr* system.

The city's physical and social organization reflected this complex relationship between public and private and between individual and group: physically separated quarters; multiple markets and mosques; mazelike patterns of narrow streets and alleys with dwellings oriented toward an inner courtyard; an absence of public meeting places other than bath, market, and mosque; and the concentration of social life in private residences. The *qāḍī* and *adīb* al-Tanūkhī provides a lively and humorous picture of 10th-century Baghdad, of a society of individuals with overlapping affiliations and shifting statuses: saints and scoundrels, heroes and rogues, rich men and poor. This mobility is illustrated by al-Tanūkhī's boast to a rival, "My line begins with me while yours ends with you." The prose genre of *maqāmah*, said to have been invented by al-Hamadhānī (died 1008), recounted the exploits of a clever, articulate scoundrel dependent on his own wits for his survival and success.

IRAN, AFGHANISTAN, AND INDIA

In the middle of the "Shīʿite century" a major Sunni revival occurred in eastern Islamdom in connection with the emergence of the second major language of Islamicate high culture, New Persian. This double revival was accomplished by two Iranian dynasties, the Sāmānids and the Ghaznavids; Ghaznavid zeal even spilled over into India.

THE SĀMĀNIDS

The Sāmānid dynasty (819–999) stemmed from a local family appointed by the ʿAbbāsids to govern at Bukhara and Samarkand. Gradually the Sāmānids had absorbed the domains of the rebellious Ṭāhirids and Ṣaffārids in northeastern Iran and reduced the Ṣaffārids to a small state in Sīstān. The Sāmānids, relying on Turkic slave troops, also managed to contain the migratory pastoralist Turkic tribes who continually pressed on Iran from across the Oxus River. In the 950s they even managed to convert some of these Turkic tribes to Islam.

The Sāmānid court at Bukhara attracted leading scholars, such as the philosophers Abū Bakr al-Rāzī (died 925 or 935) and Avicenna (Ibn Sīnā; 980–1037), who later worked for the Būyids; and the poet Ferdowsī (died c. 1020). Though not Shīʿites, the Sāmānids expressed an interest in Shīʿite thought, especially in its Ismāʿīlī form, which was then the locus of so much intellectual vitality. The Sāmānids also fostered the development of a second Islamicate language of high culture, New Persian. It combined the grammatical structure and vocabulary of spoken Persian with vocabulary from Arabic, the existing language of high culture in Iran. A landmark of this "Persianizing" of Iran was Ferdowsī's epic poem, the *Shāh-nāmeh* ("Book of Kings"), written entirely in New Persian in a long-couplet form (*masnavi*) derived from Arabic. Covering several thousand years of detailed mythic Iranian history, Ferdowsī brought Iran's ancient heroic lore, and its hero Rustam, into Islamicate literature and into the identity of self-consciously Iranian Muslims. He began to compose the poem under the rule of the Sāmānids; but he dedicated

Royal mausoleum of the Sāmānids, completed before 942 CE, Bukhara, Uzbekistan.

the finished work to a dynasty that had meanwhile replaced them, the Ghaznavids.

THE GHAZNAVIDS

The Ghaznavid dynasty was born in a way that had become routine for Islamicate polities. Sebüktigin (ruled 977–997), a Sāmānid Turkic slave governor in Ghazna (now Ghaznī), in the Afghan mountains, made himself independent of his masters as their central power declined. His eldest son, Maḥmūd, expanded into Būyid territory in western Iran, identifying himself staunchly with Sunni Islam. Presenting himself as a frontier warrior against the pagans, Maḥmūd invaded and plundered northwestern India, establishing a permanent rule in the Punjab, but it was through ruling Iran, which gave a Muslim ruler true prestige, that Maḥmūd sought to establish himself. He declared his loyalty to the ʿAbbāsid caliph, whose "investiture" he sought, and expressed his intention to defend Sunni Islam against the Shīʿite Būyids. Although he and his regime were proud of their Turkic descent, Maḥmūd encouraged the use of New Persian, with its echoes of pre-Islamic Iranian glory, for administration and for prose as well as poetry. This combination of Turkic identity and Persian language would characterize and empower many other Muslim rulers.

To Ghazna Maḥmūd brought, sometimes by force, writers and artisans who could adorn his court. Among these was al-Bīrūnī (973–c. 1050), whose scholarly achievements no contemporary could rival. Before being brought to Ghazna, al-Bīrūnī had served the Sāmānids and the Khwārazm-Shāhs, a local dynasty situated just west of the Oxus River. Al-Bīrūnī's works included studies of astronomy (he even suggested a heliocentric universe), gems, drugs, mathematics, and physics, but his most famous book, inspired by accompanying

Maḥmūd of Ghazna is shown receiving a decorated robe from the Abbāsid caliph al-Qādir in Rashīd al-Dīn's *Jāmi' al-tawārīkh* ("Collector of Chronicles")

Maḥmūd on his Indian campaigns, was a survey of Indian life, language, religion, and culture.

Like most other rulers of the day, Maḥmūd styled himself an emir and emphasized his loyalty to the caliph in Baghdad, but he and later Ghaznavid rulers also called themselves by the Arabic word *sulṭān*. Over the next five centuries the office of sultan would become an alternative to caliph. The Ghaznavid state presaged other changes as well, especially by stressing the cleavage between ruler and ruled and by drawing into the ruling class not only the military but also the bureaucracy and the learned establishment. So tied was the ruling establishment to the ruler that it even moved with him on campaign. Ghaznavid "political theory" shared with other states the concept of the

SULTAN

The title Sultan (in Arabic: *Sulṭān*) was originally used in the Qur᾿ān to denote a moral or spiritual authority. However, the term later came to denote political or governmental power and from the 11th century was used as a title by Muslim sovereigns. Maḥmūd of Ghazna was the first Muslim ruler to be called sultan by his contemporaries, and under the Seljuqs of Anatolia and Iran it became a regular title. Thereafter it was frequently conferred on sovereigns by the caliph (titular head of the Muslim community) and came to be used throughout the Islamic world.

circle of justice or circle of power—i.e., that justice is best preserved by an absolute monarch completely outside society; that such a ruler needs an absolutely loyal army; and that maintaining such an army requires prosperity, which in turn depends on the good management of an absolute ruler.

Abū al-Faḍl Bayhaqī (995–1077) worked in the Ghaznavid chancery and wrote a remarkable history of the Ghaznavids, the first major prose work in New Persian. He exhibited the broad learning of even a relatively minor figure at court; in his history he combined the effective writing skills of the chancery employee, the special knowledge of Qur᾿ān and Hadith, and the sophisticated and entertaining literature—history, poetry, and folklore—that characterized the *adīb*. He provided a vivid picture of life at court, graphically portraying the pitfalls of military absolutism—the dependence of the monarch on a fractious military and a large circle of assistants and advisors, who could mislead him and affect his decision making through internecine maneuvering and competition. In the reign of Maḥmūd's son, Masʿūd I, the weaknesses in the system had already become glaringly apparent. At the Battle of Dandānqān (1040), Masʿūd lost control of Khorāsān, his main holding in Iran, to the pastoralist Seljuq Turks; he then decided to withdraw to Lahore in his Indian domains, from which his successors ruled until overtaken by the Ghūrids in 1186.

The Decline of the Caliphate and Rise of Emirates

By the end of Masʿūd's reign, government in Islamdom had become government by emir. Caliphal centralization had lasted 200 years; even after the caliphal empire became too large and complex to be ruled from a single centre, the separate emirates that replaced it all defined their legitimacy in relation to it, for or against. In fact, the caliphate's first systematic description and justification was undertaken just when its impracticality was being demonstrated. As the Ghaznavids were ruling in Iran as "appointed" defenders of the caliph, a Baghdadi legal scholar named al-Māwardī (died 1058) retrospectively delineated the minimal requirements of the caliphate and tried to explain why it had become necessary for caliphal powers to be "delegated" in order for the *ummah's* security to be maintained. Whereas earlier legists had tied the caliph's legitimacy to his defense of the borders, al-Māwardī separated the two, maintaining the caliph as the ultimate source of legitimacy and the guardian of pan-Islamic concerns and relegating day-to-day government to his "appointees." Al-Māwardī may have hoped that the Ghaznavids would expand far enough to be "invited" by the caliph to replace the uninvited Shīʿite Būyids. This replacement did occur, three years before al-Māwardī's death; however, it was not the Ghaznavids who appeared in Baghdad but rather the migratory pastoralist Turks who had meanwhile replaced them. The Seljuqs joined many other migrating groups to produce the next phase of Islamicate history.

CONCLUSION

In its first four centuries Islam spread from a single prophet in Mecca to devout followers spread across the entirety of the Arabian Peninsula, eastward into Persia and India, north into Turkey and Central Asia, and westward along coastal areas of the Mediterranean Sea including a European foothold in Andalusia. Followers of Islam engaged in trade and travel, promoted artistic and scientific endeavors, and supported local artists as well as educators, scientists, and mathematicians. Economic growth expanded. In a relatively short period of time, Islam achieved a far-reaching religious, political, and cultural impact on a variety of civilizations.

However, the combined effect of time and geographic growth also splintered the Islamic community; numerous, competing schools of thought emerged; different political dynasties rose and fell; what was once a community of Arabs who collectively spoke Arabic became a diverse community speaking various local languages. To exacerbate rivalry and conflict between different dynasties was the rather informal nature of Islamic government, which consisted primarily of a caliph (or later, emir), his close advisors, and an army. Social problems were often dealt with locally. Very rarely was the government involved in settling familial or community disputes. Many grievances arose regarding government corruption and rising costs of food and goods.

Into this somewhat free-flowing system of religion and government entered the Seljuqs, Turkic tribes that invaded southwestern Asia in the 11th century and eventually founded an empire that included Mesopotamia, Syria, Palestine, and most of Iran. Their influence would usher in the next chapter of Islamic history.

GLOSSARY

ABRAHAMIC Religions centred on Abraham, a biblical patriarch regarded by Jews as the founder of the Hebrew people through his son Isaac and by Muslims as the founder of the Arab peoples through his son Ishmael.

ACHAEMENID A member of the ruling house of ancient Persia from 553 BCE during the reign of Cyrus the Great to the overthrow of Darius III in 330 BCE.

ANTHROPOMORPHISM An interpretation of what is not human or personal in terms of human or personal characteristics.

BEDOUIN A nomadic Arab of the Arabian, Syrian, or North African deserts.

CAPITULATION An act of surrendering or yielding.

CENTRIFUGAL Proceeding or acting in a direction away from a center.

CENTRIPETAL Proceeding or acting in a direction toward a center.

DYNAST A person who rules a country, area, group, etc.

ENTREPÔT A place serving as an intermediary center for the collection and distribution of goods.

EXCLUSIVISTIC Characterized by a limitation to possession, control, or use by a single individual or group.

GNOSTICISM The thought and practice especially of various cults of late pre-Christian and early Christian centuries distinguished by the conviction that matter is evil and that emancipation comes through gnosis (esoteric knowledge of spiritual truth).

ISLAMDOM Of or relating to the complex of societies in which Muslims and their faith have been prevalent and socially dominant.

ISLAMICATE Of or relating to the social and cultural complex that is historically associated with Islam and Muslims, even when found among non-Muslims.

LINGUA FRANCA A language that is used among people who speak various different languages.

MANICHAEISM A syncretistic religious dualism originating in Persia by the prophet Mani, which teaches that a cosmic conflict exists between a good realm of light and an evil realm of darkness.

MONOPHYSITE One holding the doctrine that Christ has a single inseparable nature that is at once divine and human rather than having two distinct but unified natures.

NESTORIAN Of or relating to a church separating from Byzantine Christianity after 431, centering in Persia, and surviving chiefly in Asia Minor.

OLIGARCHY A country, business, etc., that is controlled by a small group of people.

PASTORALIST Of or relating to a social organization based on livestock raising as the primary economic activity.

PHARAONIC Of, relating to, or characteristic of a pharaoh or of ancient Egypt in general.

PHILOLOGIAN One that is learned or literary.

QUIETISTIC Of or relating to a system of religious mysticism that teaches that perfection and spiritual peace are attained by annihilation of the will and passive absorption in contemplation of God and divine things.

RECENSION A text established by critical revision.

SACRALIZATION The process of treating or making something sacred.

SĀSĀNIAN Of, relating to, or having the characteristics of the dynasty of Persian kings of the 3rd to 7th centuries CE.

SEDENTARIZATION The process of becoming settled and no longer migratory.

TROIKA A group of three.

UNITIVE Characterized by or tending to produce union.

BIBLIOGRAPHY

Surveys

The most visionary general work on Islamic history is Marshall G.S. Hodgson, *The Venture of Islam: Conscience and History in a World Civilization*, 3 vol. (1974), which sets Islam into a world historical context. A similar but shorter work, sumptuously illustrated, is Francis Robinson, *Atlas of the Islamic World Since 1500* (1982).

Regions of Islamdom

Peter B. Clarke, *West Africa and Islam: A Study of Religious Development from the 8th to the 20th Centuries* (1982); Jamil M. Abun-Nasr, *A History of the Maghrib*, 2nd ed. (1975); Clifford Geertz, *Islam Observed: Religious Development in Morocco and Indonesia* (1968, reissued 1971); S.M. Ikram, *Muslim Rule in India and Pakistan, 711–1858 A.C.*, rev. ed. (1966); Raphael Israeli, *Muslims in China: A Study in Cultural Confrontation* (1980); and Nehemia Levtzion (ed.), *Conversion to Islam* (1979).

Periods and Aspects of Islamicate History

Premodern Islamicate social structure is treated in Roy P. Mottahedeh, *Loyalty and Leadership in an Early Islamic Society* (1980); and S.D. Goitein, *A Mediterranean Society: The Jewish Communities of the Arab World as Portrayed in the Documents of the Cairo Geniza*, 4 vol. (1967–83). Hamilton A.R. Gibb, *Studies on the Civilization of Islam* (1962, reissued 1982), is a collection of interpretive articles on history, historiography, literature, and philology.

Collections of Primary Sources in English Translation

Eric Schroeder, *Muhammad's People* (1955); Arthur Jeffery (ed.), *A Reader of Isla*m (1962, reprinted 1980); John Alden Williams (ed.), *Islam* (1961, reissued 1967), and *Themes of Islamic Civilization* (1971, reprinted 1982); William H. McNeill and Marilyn Robinson Waldman, *The Islamic World* (1973, reprinted 1983); James Kritzeck, *Anthology of Islamic Literature* (1964, reissued 1975); and Bernard Lewis (ed.), I*slam: From the Prophet Muhammad to the Capture of Constantinople,* 2 vol. (1974, reissued 1976).

Major Reference Works

The Encyclopaedia of Islam, 5 vol. (1913–36), and a new edition, of which 5 vol. appeared from 1960 to 1986; *The Shorter Encyclopaedia of Islam* (1953, reprinted 1974), with articles culled from the *Encyclopaedia of Islam; The Cambridge History of Islam*, 2 vol. (1970, reprinted in 4 vol., 1980); Jean Sauvaget, *Jean Sauvaget's Introduction to the History of the Muslim East: A Bibliographical Guide* (1965, reprinted 1982; originally published in French, 2nd ed., 1961), a dated but still useful annotated bibliographic guide; Clifford Edmund Bosworth, *The Islamic Dynasties: A Chronological and Genealogical Handboo*k, rev. ed. (1980); and *Encyclopedia of Women and Islamic Culture*s, 6 vol. (2003, 2005–07). Jean Jacques Waardenburg, *L'Islam dans le miroir de l'Occiden*t, 3rd rev. ed. (1970); and Edward W. Said, *Orientalism* (1978, reissued 1979), are critiques of Western approaches to Islam.

INDEX